UNDERSTANDING
THE
TWELVE STEPS

UNDERSTANDING

THE

TWELVE STEPS

*An Interpretation and Guide
for Recovering People*

T. Terence T. Gorski

A FIRESIDE BOOK
Published by Simon & Schuster
New York London Toronto Sydney

F

FIRESIDE

Rockefeller Center
1230 Avenue of the Americas
New York, New York 10020

Copyright © 1989 by Terence T. Gorski

All rights reserved,
including the right of reproduction
in whole or in part in any form

FIRESIDE and colophon are registered trademarks
of Simon & Schuster Inc.

Originally published by Herald House/Independence Press
Designed by Irving Perkins Associates

Manufactured in the United States of America

31 33 35 37 39 40 38 36 34 32

First Prentice Hall Press Edition 1991
First Fireside Edition 1992

Library of Congress Cataloging-in-Publication Data

Gorski, Terence T.
Understanding the twelve steps / Terence Gorski.
p.   cm.
1. Alcoholics—Rehabilitation.   2. Alcoholics Anonymous.
I. Title.   II. Title: Understanding the 12 steps.
HV5278.G67   1991
362.29'286—dc20   89-77134
ISBN-13: 978-0-671-76558-3   CIP
ISBN-10:   0-671-76558-2

This book is dedicated to Father Joseph Martin,
whose tireless efforts in carrying the message
have enhanced the sobriety of many.

ACKNOWLEDGMENTS

This book is being written in an effort to give back some of the knowledge, wisdom, and love that have been shared with me so freely in the course of my life.

I am especially grateful to the mentors Stan Martindale and Richard Weedman, who became my professional role models. It was Richard Weedman who first introduced me to the Twelve Steps and their power in keeping alcoholics sober. Jim Kelleher, my friend and first clinical supervisor, gave me direct experience with how the program works in the real world.

I am grateful to my wife, Jan Smith, who has provided love and caring throughout this project, and to Joseph Troiani, my lifelong friend and colleague, who supported me in the writing effort.

I would also like to thank Christina Carlson, who is responsible for transcribing the original manuscript from a workshop tape and helping me shape that into the final book.

Mary Lou Nylen and Karen Plath were helpful in typing and retyping the manuscript. Janet Voss helped in reviewing the final manuscript.

My literary agent, Candice Fuhrman, has provided help and support in making this book possible. Without her efforts to seek me out and encourage me in the writing effort, this book would not have been possible.

CONTENTS

INTRODUCTION

This is a book about the Twelve Steps of Alcoholics Anonymous and the principles upon which they are based. I was initially reluctant to write this book because there is a wealth of information available on the Twelve Steps, and I didn't feel my personal interpretation was necessary or valuable.

My attitude changed in the late 1980s after doing a series of workshops on the Twelve Steps for professional counselors and therapists. Although the workshops originally were designed for psychotherapists who had no direct A.A. involvement, many counselors with long-term sobriety and in-depth experience with Twelve Step programs attended. In private conversations, many encouraged me to publish my perspective on the Steps because they felt that it provided a practical, rational, and no-nonsense approach to a philosophy that often is vague and difficult to understand. This book is the result of that encouragement.

I was further encouraged by my association with Father Joseph Martin, the creator of the film *Chalk Talk* and cofounder of Ashley, a treatment center in Havre de Grace, Maryland, based in large part on the Twelve Steps. My understanding of the Twelve Steps has been heavily influenced by Father Martin and my ongoing association with Ashley. In many ways, this book as it is written today would not have been possible without the information and wisdom that Father Martin so freely shared with me.

In this book I approach the Steps from both a professional and a personal perspective. As a professional, my approach is based on more than twenty years of experience as an alcoholism and drug-abuse counselor, with additional experience in research, clinical administration, consultation, and training. After having worked with recovering alcoholics who have organized their lives around the Twelve Steps, it is impossible not to have been personally affected by this philosophy of life.

I need to make an important disclaimer. This book presents my personal opinions about the Twelve Steps and Twelve Step organizations. I am in no way speaking for or authorized to represent A.A. or any other Twelve Step program. My primary purpose is to share my experience in an effort to help others recover.

Being a fallible human being, my grasp of the Twelve Steps is incomplete at best. It is my hope that some of the concepts in this book will be helpful to you in your recovery. As you read this book, take for yourself the information you find helpful and leave the rest behind.

—Terence T. Gorski

UNDERSTANDING
THE
TWELVE STEPS

1

WHAT IS A TWELVE STEP PROGRAM?

This book describes the single, most effective program for the treatment of alcoholism. That program, of course, is Alcoholics Anonymous, best known as A.A. Alcoholics Anonymous is a worldwide fellowship of men and women who share their experience, strength, and hope with each other in an effort to recover from alcoholism. It is a voluntary fellowship. No one is forced to belong, but millions of voluntary members benefit greatly from their involvement. If you want to make Twelve Step programs work for you, you need to understand the fellowship of A.A. and how to work with it. This book is intended to help you do just that.

Many people find the miracle of sobriety by working the Twelve Steps. Since nothing else has worked for them, many believe that the Steps are mystical and magical, and, as a result, these same persons fail to search for and identify the underlying principles that make them work. Working the Steps can create the miracle of sobriety, but the miracle isn't magic. The miracle occurs because working the Twelve Steps allows people to use powerful principles of recovery. Those who are willing to dig beneath the surface and truly understand the principles upon which the Steps are based are better able to use the principles in their lives.

The primary purpose of A.A. is to help alcoholics stop drinking. It was never intended to be all things to all people; however, A.A. recognizes that the Twelve Steps can help people with other problems. Thus, it allows organizations such as Narcotics Anonymous, Cocaine Anonymous, Marijuana Anonymous, Overeaters Anonymous, and others to use its Steps and principles. These related fellowships are developing as separate organizations so that A.A. can keep its primary focus on helping alcoholics to stop drinking.

A.A. is based upon a program of Twelve Steps to recovery that act as a personal guide to sobriety, and Twelve Traditions that act as guiding principles or bylaws for A.A. as a whole. Knowledge of the Twelve Steps is of critical importance to all recovering people for two reasons: (1) The Steps work if you work them, and (2) Twelve Step programs are inexpensive and readily available in most communities. As a result, they are the most widely used lifeline for people recovering from chemical dependence, codependence, and other compulsive or addictive disorders.

A.A. AS A NONPROFESSIONAL GROUP

As a result of the Traditions, A.A. is and shall forever remain nonprofessional. There are no medical professionals, as such, involved in designing or running A.A. or other Twelve Step programs. Although medical professionals do join as members, they have no more or no less influence on the organization than other members. Twelve Step programs do not provide medical or psychiatric treatment or psychotherapy. If you are involved in any Twelve Step program that has a psychotherapist in charge who runs it like a therapy group, be cautious. You are probably not at a Twelve Step meeting. This situation rarely, if ever, occurs in A.A.; however, it does happen in some of the newer Twelve Step programs.

If you are attending a Twelve Step meeting that is run by a psychotherapist who individually counsels the members, it is not a Twelve Step meeting; it is a therapy group. It is important to learn the difference, because Twelve Step meetings are based on the Twelve Steps of A.A. and the leaders act in a nonprofessional role.

A.A. members help themselves and others to stay sober. Members can be assured that they are not going to be solicited for donations or asked to get involved in anything else. Individual members of A.A. do have the right to participate in any religion, political forum, or cause that they wish. There are no restrictions. But they are not allowed to present themselves as A.A. members or to bring the name of A.A. into any controversy.

LEVELS OF TWELVE STEP INVOLVEMENT

Nobody is forced to do anything in A.A. It is one of the few organizations I know that supports the inherent constitutional right to do what we want. There is no coercion to participate on any level. If you want to belong, that's fine. You are welcome to attend meetings and work the Steps. If you don't want to belong, that's also fine.

For most members, however, their involvement progresses through a number of levels. At the first level, they attend meetings. At the second, they read Twelve Step literature and discuss it with other members of the program. At the third level, they get a sponsor who can show them how the program works. At the fourth level, they start working the Twelve Steps. As members start to grow and change—a result of attending meetings and working the Steps—they are ready to move to a fifth level of involvement and begin sponsoring others. After they gain experience as sponsors, they are then ready for the sixth level of involvement, general service work, guided by A.A.'s Twelve Traditions, the set of principles that act as bylaws. General service work is designed to benefit A.A. as a whole. Notice the progression: Individuals help themselves first, then they help other people in the program, then they help the program as a whole. In summary, the levels of involvement are as follows:

1. Attending meetings
2. Reading and discussing A.A. literature
3. Getting a sponsor
4. Working the Twelve Steps
5. Sponsoring others
6. Service guided by the Traditions

ATTENDING MEETINGS

You start working a Twelve Step program by regularly attending meetings. In A.A. it is said, "If you bring the body, the mind will follow," because the Twelve Step program rubs off on people if they hang around long enough. Attending meetings isn't a passive process. Working a program means you need to get actively involved, participating at the meetings you attend. The easiest way to take part is to say, "I pass"—a perfectly acceptable remark. No one in a Twelve Step program is obligated to say more. Most people, however, want to say more because they find it both enjoyable and beneficial. The more open and honest your comments, the faster you get well.

There is a joke that asks, "What is the difference between a drunk and an alcoholic?" Answer: "A drunk doesn't have to go to meetings; an alcoholic does!" A.A. stresses the importance of attending meetings, especially during the first three months of sobriety. Many members suggest attending ninety meetings in ninety days. By doing "ninety in ninety," beginners receive an intense exposure to the Twelve Step program and the people who use it. The principle that underlies doing "ninety in ninety" is a simple one— the more meetings you attend early on, the greater your chances of long-term recovery. There is no rule, of course, that you have to attend exactly ninety meetings in the first ninety days; go as often as your lifestyle allows. But keep in mind that the more meetings you attend, the faster you will get well.

Many members complain about having to attend meetings, but those who recover keep going even when they don't feel like it. You don't have to like going to meetings, you just have to keep going. Meetings are the lifeline to sobriety. When you attend meetings, you take a needed time-out from an alcohol- and drug-centered world and remind yourself that you are an alcoholic, cannot safely use alcohol and other drugs, and that you need the fellowship of other sober alcoholics to stay sober.

READING TWELVE STEP LITERATURE

The second level of involvement is to read Twelve Step literature and discuss your reactions, both positive and negative, with other members. The early members of A.A. identified the basic principles needed to get sober and stay that way. They compiled that information in two books—

Alcoholics Anonymous (often called the Big Book) and *Twelve Steps and Twelve Traditions*. Both books are available from the central office of Alcoholics Anonymous in New York City. These books provide the basic principles needed to begin living the sober life.

GETTING A SPONSOR

After you feel comfortable going to meetings, making comments, and reading the basic literature, the third level of involvement is to get a sponsor. A sponsor is another member of the Twelve Step program who has more experience at recovery than you do. In order to get a sponsor, you must have participated in the program long enough to get to know people. Listen to the comments of others. Try to find someone you respect and admire, someone who knows more than you do about the program and can show you the ropes. In the business world, a sponsor is called a mentor.

When you find such a person and ask him or her to be your sponsor, you are in essence asking, "Would you be willing to spend time with me and teach me how you work the program?" There's a slogan in the Twelve Step program: "If you want what we have, you do what we did." And it's primarily in the sponsorship relationship that this principle comes alive. You find a sponsor who has the type of recovery you would like to have, ask him to teach you what steps he took, and then try to do those things in your recovery.

A therapist does not take the place of a sponsor. You need a Twelve Step sponsor even if you have the best therapist in the world. A good therapist will encourage recovering people to become involved in Twelve Step programs and to get a sponsor. As a therapist, I don't mandate Twelve Step attendance, but I do strongly encourage it. If someone refuses to attend even one meeting to see what the organization is all about, I may say, "If you're not willing to go to Twelve Step meetings, I'm not willing to treat you. Why? Because if you're not willing to go and find out what Twelve Step programs involve, I don't think you really want to do what's necessary to recover." I base this attitude on an A.A. slogan: "We must be willing to go to any lengths to get sober." If you are not willing to clear a few evenings and attend some meetings, I question your willingness to do what is necessary to recover.

WORK THE STEPS

Once you have a solid relationship with a good sponsor, you move to the fourth level: working the Twelve Steps. Step work under the guidance of a sponsor is literally the heart and soul of most Twelve Step programs, and the bulk of this book deals with how to work the Steps. Members who go to meetings but refuse to work the Steps are not really working the program. To quote the Big Book, "Rarely have we seen a person fail who has thoroughly followed our path." People who genuinely want to recover do more than just go to meetings: They work the Steps under the guidance of their sponsor. Those who are not serious about recovery don't work the steps. It's just that simple.

SPONSORING OTHERS

By attending meetings, reading Twelve Step literature, talking frequently with sponsors, and working the Steps, you begin to grow and change. The program will start to transform you. As you learn and grow, you need to reach out and start giving back to others what has been given to you so freely. In short, it is time to move onto the fifth level and begin sponsoring others.

Sponsorship has two purposes: to help yourself and to help the person you sponsor. It is important to remember that you sponsor others in order to help yourself. You are in no way responsible for the recovery or relapse of the people you sponsor. The primary goal is to share freely your own experience, strength, and hope, and by doing so, you help yourself and may help the person you are sponsoring. But there are no guarantees. A.A. is a selfish program: Recovering people help others in order to help themselves. This attitude is clearly summed up in an A.A. slogan: "In order to keep it, you have to give it away."

By pairing with someone who is less experienced with the Twelve Steps than you are, and by trying to help him or her, you gain new insights into your own recovery. When I first started teaching courses on counseling, I realized how much I didn't know. I became motivated to learn more. The same is true in sponsorship. When you try to answer the questions of a newcomer, you become aware of your own ignorance. You gain the courage to stretch and to grow. When someone you are sponsoring asks you a question and you don't know the answer, it is time to go to your own sponsor. By helping others, we have been forced to learn. The formula is simple: Attend meetings, work the Steps, have a sponsor, and sponsor others.

SERVICE GUIDED BY THE TRADITIONS

The sixth level of involvement is service guided by the Traditions. Every organization needs bylaws, and Twelve Step programs are no exception. The twelve fundamental bylaws that govern the operation of Twelve Step programs are called the Traditions. There is a need to maintain the organization of a Twelve Step program in order to make sure that the program continues to be available to help others. It is important to keep first things first. Service work is secondary to working the Steps and learning how to stay comfortable in recovery. But once A.A. members have a firm handle on their own recovery, service work is important to ensure the survival of the organization as a whole.

IN ORDER TO KEEP IT, YOU HAVE TO GIVE IT AWAY

Father Joseph Martin, the creator of the film *Chalk Talk* and cofounder of the Ashley treatment center in Havre de Grace, Maryland, told me this story of A.A.'s cofounder, Bill Wilson. Bill tried to stay sober all by himself for a long period of time, but he could never manage more than a few weeks of sobriety. Then he had this crazy notion that maybe he could help himself stay sober by helping other people to stay sober. The first approach Bill tried was what I call the "scrape them off the bar stool" approach. He talked to all of his friends with drinking problems and tried to convince them to stop. Basically, he went on a crusade to sober up drunks. Six months later, he told his wife, Lois, "I've failed. I've been trying to help alcoholics now for six months, and I haven't helped one person to get sober." Lois looked at him and said, "Bill, you're wrong. You have helped someone. *You* haven't had a drink in six months." Thus, one of the first principles of A.A. was born. It is summarized in the slogan, "In order to keep it, you have to give it away." The benefit of A.A. is that its members, recovering people in Twelve Step programs, get well by helping others to get well.

9

By trying to help others, people in recovery transcend their own selfishness; they interrupt the self-centeredness that is central to most addictions and compulsions. By trying to help others, addicts no longer remain the central part of their own personal addictive network. They begin to expand their world beyond the tip of their nose. In doing so, they find new values to govern their lives.

A.A. provides a number of crystal-clear guidelines: Don't drink, go to meetings, get a sponsor, work the Steps. Beyond these basics, there is a lot of ambiguity. After reading A.A. literature or attending a meeting, it is common for a member to scratch his or her head and ask, "What does that mean?" Part of the power of A.A. lies in this ambiguity, which forces people to provide their own meaning when working the program. Recovering people must make up their own minds and decide what the A.A. principles mean for them. One of the hallmarks of A.A. is that it's a "selfish" program. Members decide for themselves what they take out of the meetings. Nobody tells them what their experience is. They take what fits them and they leave the rest.

THE TRADITIONS

Knowledge of the Traditions is important because these simple bylaws protect A.A. as a whole.

The First Tradition reads: "Our common welfare should come first; personal recovery depends upon A.A. unity." If the Fellowship of A.A. is destroyed, nobody gets sober. So when any decisions are made about A.A. as a whole, the common welfare of the organization is the primary concern.

The Second Tradition is: "For our group purpose there is but one ultimate authority—a loving God as He may express Himself in our group conscience. Our leaders are but trusted servants; they do not govern." There are no leaders of A.A. Each group is governed by group conscience, the consensus of the group. The leaders in A.A. are but trusted servants of this group conscience. Since there is no centralized leadership, anyone who chooses to become active can influence the group. The organizational structure has but one purpose: to determine what the group conscience is and to act accordingly.

The Third Tradition is: "The only requirement for A.A. membership is a desire to stop drinking." Anyone who says, "I want to stop drinking" can get in. That's the only requirement.

The Fourth Tradition reads: "Each group should be autonomous except in matters affecting other groups or A.A. as a whole." Each group is autonomous and operates based upon its own group conscience. If you attend an A.A. meeting and don't like what is going on, you can call a group conscience meeting and discuss the situation. If you are in a minority and nobody else wants to do what you want to do, you have a right to go and start your own A.A. meeting someplace else.

The Fifth Tradition states: "Each group has but one primary purpose—to carry its message to the alcoholic who still suffers." Notice that the Tradition specifies "alcoholic"; it doesn't say "chemically dependent person." There are other self-help groups, such as Narcotics Anonymous (N.A.), Cocaine Anonymous (C.A.), and so on, to help people whose drug of choice is something other than alcohol. A.A.'s primary purpose is to help alcoholics. Although many A.A. members are addicted to other drugs as well as alcohol, A.A.'s only requirement for membership is

11

a desire to stop drinking, and its primary purpose is to carry the message of recovery to alcoholics who still suffer.

The Sixth Tradition is: "An A.A. group ought never endorse, finance, or lend the A.A. name to any related facility or outside enterprise, lest problems of money, property, and prestige divert us from our primary purpose." A.A. groups don't endorse, finance, or lend the A.A. name to any outside causes to avoid being diverted from their primary purpose of helping other alcoholics. In some communities, members of A.A. and nonmember friends of the program form nonprofit corporations or foundations that may purchase or rent buildings that they use as social clubs and meeting places. These clubs are not affiliated in any way with A.A. That's why A.A. has survived for so long. A.A. does one thing—it helps alcoholics achieve sobriety. And that's what it does best!

The Seventh Tradition states: "Every A.A. group ought to be fully self-supporting, declining outside contributions." Each group supports itself through the contributions of its own members and declines contributions from any outside source.

The Eighth Tradition states: "Alcoholics Anonymous should remain forever nonprofessional, but our service centers may employ special workers." Although A.A. is nonprofessional, most large cities do have a small service office with a telephone number for people to call who need help. Local A.A. groups contribute part of their weekly donations to support these typically modest facilities. Service centers can hire staff if that seems appropriate, but most of them are manned by volunteers.

The Ninth Tradition is: "A.A. as such, ought never be organized; but we may create service boards or committees directly responsible to those they serve." A.A. is not a traditional organization whose leaders control it from the

WHAT IS A TWELVE STEP PROGRAM?

top down. It is a network whose members run it from the bottom up. A.A.'s "government" is kept simple to avoid building a self-serving bureaucracy. This simplicity keeps control of the organization where it belongs—in the hands of the recovering alcoholics who are attending meetings.

In various areas there are regional elected officers and regional service boards designed to meet the needs of local groups. Groups elect representatives, who meet to plan and coordinate such activities as public information workshops and regional conferences. They are not a required or mandated part of the Fellowship, and they can be voted in or out of existence.

The Tenth Tradition states: "Alcoholics Anonymous has no opinion on outside issues; hence the A.A. name ought never be drawn into public controversy." A.A. has no opinions on anything except A.A. If somebody says A.A. thinks this or that, they are wrong—unless they are saying that A.A. thinks there should be Twelve Steps and Twelve Traditions and that alcoholics should not drink. Those are stances that A.A. takes for the benefit of its members. A.A., as an organization, has opinions only on the issue of helping alcoholics.

The Eleventh Tradition reads: "Our public relations policy is based on attraction rather than promotion; we need always maintain personal anonymity at the level of press, radio, and films." A.A. does not advertise or promote its program of recovery in any way. Instead, it attracts new members by the example set by the thousands of people who are sober as a result of participation in the fellowship. To avoid advertising or promoting A.A., members should never disclose in the press, on radio, or in films that they are members.

The Twelfth Tradition states: "Anonymity is the spiritual foundation of all our traditions, ever reminding us to place principles before personalities." The maintenance of anonymity is very important. The goal is to avoid having the A.A. program associated with any single personality or celebrity. A.A. as an organization is bigger than any of its individual members. The goal is to put principles before personalities.

THE TREND TOWARD SELF-CARE

Twelve Step groups are everywhere—or so it seems. Alcoholics Anonymous, starting with its quiet beginnings in 1935, has emerged as a major influence that is shaping the future of America. John Naisbitt, a man who earns his living by analyzing future trends, confirms that A.A. and other self-help groups are part of a major national trend from professional care to self-care.

In the past, most Americans turned to professionals for help and support when things went wrong. But all that is changing as people take control of and responsibility for their own lives. Growing numbers of people are turning to self-help support groups as their primary source of assistance when trouble hits. Many of these groups are based upon the Twelve Steps of A.A.

There is a "statement of responsibility" in A.A. that says, "Anytime, anyone, anywhere reaches out for help, the hand of A.A. will be there, for this I am responsible." The incredible thing about this is that most A.A. members mean it! Any alcoholic who calls A.A. is referred to another member who gets that person to a meeting and orients him or her to the program. There is no charge for this highly personalized service. It happens because one alcoholic who feels that A.A. has saved his or her life is returning the favor to another alcoholic. The same is true in most other Twelve Step fellowships. Why? Because it is part of the program. Remember: "In order to keep it, you have to give it away!"

The popularity of A.A. and the Twelve Steps is not a fad. The Twelve Step philosophy is emerging as a powerful social trend. The Twelve Step movement is slowly creating a new way of thinking—one person at a time, one day at a time, in a very "easy does it" manner. The number of A.A. spin-off groups that use the Twelve Steps is growing every day. Al-Anon was the first such group designed to help people who were affected by the alcoholism of another. Adult Children of Alcoholics (ACoA) is another major spin-off of A.A. As America moved into the age of "better living through chemistry," a number of other drug-addiction recovery groups, such as Narcotics Anonymous, Marijuana Anonymous, Cocaine Anonymous, and Pills Anonymous, were begun for people whose primary drug of choice is one other than alcohol. There are also Overeaters Anonymous, Gamblers Anonymous, Families Anonymous, Emotions Anonymous, and more than 200 other Twelve Step recovery groups. We are seeing a very powerful self-care movement that is readily available in most communities throughout the world.

In order to recover, chemically dependent people need to understand how to access the power of this movement to recover. Twelve Step groups provide a powerful source of information, courage, strength, and hope. And even though they will never totally replace professional care, these Twelve Step programs can be an effective, low-cost, and readily available adjunct to professional treatment.

Because A.A. is the single, most effective way to recover from chemical dependence, I strongly recommend it to all recovering people. If someone were to say to me, "I am only willing to do one thing for recovery. What should I do?" my answer as a professional counselor would be: "Go to A.A." Why? Because A.A. as a single, stand-alone source of help, is the most effective means of getting sober. There are more people sober as a result of attending A.A. and nothing else, than there are people who participate in all other forms of counseling and therapy combined. A.A. is by far the most powerful and most readily available recovery resource.

2

THE "TWELVE STEP PLUS" APPROACH

Many alcoholics need more help than A.A. alone can provide. It is common for recovering people to struggle with depression, anxiety, relationship problems, eating disorders, and other problems that can jeopardize their sobriety. They can't afford to ignore these problems or other sources of help that may be necessary to cope with them. The Twelve Step program advises that you must be willing to go to any lengths to get sober and stay that way. And "any lengths" often means getting additional help from doctors, psychologists, and/or counselors. Most recovering people can benefit from both the Twelve Steps and professional therapy. I call this the "Twelve Step Plus" approach, and research clearly shows that it provides the best chance for long-term recovery.

THE EVIDENCE THAT A.A. WORKS

Research shows that A.A. works, but it works better when combined with professional counseling or therapy. There have been fifteen large-scale questionnaire surveys of members attending meetings of Alcoholics Anonymous, including seven studies conducted by A.A. itself. The results show that 40 to 50 percent of alcoholics who join A.A. become long-term members, and 60 to 68 percent of those long-term members achieve permanent abstinence or a decrease in the amount of time spent drinking. In an average A.A. meeting, about 35 percent of the members have been sober less than one year, 35 percent between one and five years, and the remaining 30 percent more than five years.

A.A. involvement is consistently related to improved social functioning, improved marital and family adjustment, and improved psychological adjustment. A.A. members tend to develop an active spiritual life, a greater sense of self-reliance and self-confidence, and a decreased dependence on others.

The research builds a convincing argument that A.A. in combination with professional treatment is the most effective form of help. The difference is observable from the very start. Fifty to 60 percent of the alcoholics attending only A.A. will drop out within the first ninety days. The dropout rate is cut in half for patients referred to A.A. as part of professional treatment. A.A. members who are also active in counseling and therapy relapse less frequently and achieve more comfort and peace of mind in sobriety than those who only attend A.A.

A.A. has no position for or against professional therapy, but many A.A. members have benefited from using both. For instance, Bill Wilson, one of the founders of A.A., participated in psychiatric treatment for depression after he got sober.

WHO NEEDS THE "TWELVE STEP PLUS" APPROACH?

How can you know if you need additional help? There are four indicators: severe withdrawal, physical illness, extreme confusion, and relationship problems.

SEVERE WITHDRAWAL

The first indicator is being unable to get sober because of severe withdrawal. Many people can't get sober in A.A. because they experience such severe withdrawal that they would have convulsions and die if they were to stop "cold turkey." Getting someone through this acute withdrawal has been one of A.A.'s biggest problems since its beginning in 1935. Initially, sober A.A. members would "baby-sit" with newcomers as they sweated their way through "the shakes"—since, at that time, most doctors or hospitals would not treat alcoholics. Fortunately, times have changed. Today it is relatively easy to obtain medical treatment for alcoholics in withdrawal. Most communities have treatment centers based on the "Minnesota Model of Treatment." This treatment combines detoxification and rehabilitation services with the Twelve Steps. As a result, newly sober people can receive medical supervision during withdrawal as well as intensive education and counseling. They eventually leave treatment with a head start on the Twelve Step program.

It is important to remember that A.A. does not replace the need for medical detoxification. If someone is going into severe withdrawal from alcohol or drugs, the first stop should be a hospital that specializes in the treatment of chemical dependency. Only when the person is medically stable can she or he start working a Twelve Step program.

PHYSICAL ILLNESS

The second indicator that someone might need more help than A.A. alone is the presence of serious physical illnesses sometimes caused by the addiction. The medical complications that often coexist with addiction can be fatal, and A.A. is not and never was intended to be a substitute for medical treatment. But some people don't get the point until it is too late.

Liz and Joe were both recovering alcoholics involved in A.A. Liz relapsed after three years of sobriety. Joe distrusted doctors and treatment centers, believing that A.A. was all the help that an alcoholic could ever need. Even though Liz was very sick, Joe took her to an A.A. meeting when she finally asked for help. He then took her home and decided to baby-sit with her until the shakes passed. It wasn't until she started having convulsions that Joe took her to a hospital. Liz nearly died. She never would have had a convulsion if Joe had taken her to a medically supervised alcoholism treatment center.

Father Joseph Martin is a strong supporter of A.A. He calls it the most effective therapy on earth, but he also knows its limitations. In one lecture, he said, "Ladies and gentlemen, if I walk out of this lecture hall tonight and I get hit by a truck, take me to the hospital! Don't take me to an A.A. meeting!"

Individuals need to use common sense in their approach to A.A. If someone is in withdrawal or physically ill, the first stop has to be a place that can provide appropriate medical treatment with an addiction focus.

EXTREME CONFUSION

The third factor that indicates someone needs more than just A.A. is extreme confusion, anxiety, fearfulness, inability to concentrate, or out-of-control behavior in spite of regular A.A. attendance. Many people have difficulty with the Twelve Step program because they stay confused and anxious for a long time after they get sober. They can't remember things or concentrate. Often they are out of control even when sober and attending meetings. These problems are often caused by one of two conditions—post acute withdrawal (PAW) or emotional problems.

Post acute withdrawal (PAW) is temporary brain dysfunction caused by chronic alcohol and drug poisoning. Doctors used to believe that when addicts stopped using alcohol and drugs, their brains would return to normal within a matter of days. They now know that this is not the case. About one-half of all recovering alcoholics have severe symptoms of PAW that can last for six to eighteen months into sobriety. These symptoms, caused by a toxic brain, include the inability to think clearly or manage feelings and emotions. In addition, there may be memory problems and the inability to sleep restfully. Many people find themselves feeling overwhelmed by stress and overreact to little things that happen to them. Newly sober people have often told me that they feel like they are walking around in a fog. When these PAW symptoms are severe, it is difficult for them to understand or work the Twelve Steps. Some people with severe PAW mistakenly label themselves as "constitutionally incapable" of working a program with the rigorous honesty that is required to make the Twelve Steps work.

These people need to learn how to recognize and manage PAW symptoms by working with a doctor, treatment center, or counselor who has been trained to deal with the symptoms. Until they do, their PAW will continue to interfere with working the Twelve Step program.

Emotional problems can cause symptoms that are similar to PAW. People who experience severe depression, anxiety, fear, or nervousness should be evaluated by a qualified therapist, social worker, psychologist, or psychiatrist. Select someone who understands chemical addictions, but get help. Unless treated, personality and mental disorders can lead to relapse.

RELATIONSHIP PROBLEMS

The fourth and final indicator that you need more than A.A. alone is the inability to build satisfying friendships or love relationships in sobriety. Although Twelve Step programs provide a great deal of fellowship and access to a sober social environment, the program is not designed to teach people how to build friendships or develop meaningful love relationships. It also won't help people who are homeless or who need jobs. Many in recovery need halfway houses or extended rehabilitation services just to get back on their feet. There are social service organizations designed to meet these needs.

Many alcoholics are black-and-white thinkers. They believe it's all or nothing—all A.A. or no A.A.; all therapy or no therapy. My recommendation is to break out of your "either . . . or" thinking and try both. Remember, research shows that the "Twelve Step Plus" approach will give you the best chance of long-term recovery.

3

WHAT HAPPENS AT TWELVE STEP MEETINGS?

There are two types of Twelve Step meetings—open meetings attended by both alcoholics and nonalcoholics, and closed meetings reserved for alcoholics only.

There are also many closed "specialty" meetings for doctors, nurses, pharmacists, pilots. To attend these meetings, a person must contact a recovering member of that profession. Some closed meetings are held within prisons, treatment centers, hospitals, and other institutions, and only residents can attend these.

Both open and closed meetings usually start with a lead presentation. The lead can consist of a short talk by a member who shares his or her personal experiences, an exploration of one of the Steps, the reading of some program literature, or the introduction of a general discussion topic such as "anger," "hate," "sex," or "how to deal with cravings." Typically, somebody introduces the topic by telling about his or her personal experience with that issue in recovery. Or a member may read a brief piece on the topic and then invite other members to comment.

The most important kind of meeting is your "home

group"—a meeting that you attend every week without fail. People in a home group get to know one another well. You'll be missed if you don't show up, and if you lapse back into denial, the group is able to confront you. The group members troubleshoot for one another. Many people select a member of their home group as their sponsor.

An A.A. meeting generally follows a typical format. First, there are some brief opening comments. A "secretary," elected by the group, opens the meeting by saying, "This is the so-and-so A.A. chapter of such-and-such community. We meet here regularly at this time every Tuesday night." At some meetings, members are then asked to "take a moment of silence to reflect on why we are here and what we each hope to accomplish." In many groups, this moment of reflection is followed by the Serenity Prayer, which reads: "God, grant me the serenity to accept the things I cannot change, the courage to change the things I can, and the wisdom to know the difference." This prayer focuses members upon the one thing they can control—whether or not they take a drink.

Next, some reading is included during the opening comments. The first few pages of Chapter 5 of the Big Book may be read. Somebody may read from *Twelve Steps and Twelve Traditions* or some other A.A. literature.

The opening is often followed by the welcoming of newcomers and announcements "for the good of A.A." Then the speaker, chairperson, or group leader makes a brief lead presentation for fifteen or twenty minutes. He or she shares his or her experience, strength, and hope either by telling a personal story or talking about a particular topic. Sometimes the group reviews one of the Steps or reads and discusses some conference-approved literature, such as the *Grapevine*, A.A.'s monthly magazine.

Then there is often a short break during which a collection basket is passed around, and members are reminded of A.A.'s Seventh Tradition: "A.A. is self-supporting through its own contributions." Often there is a break for coffee.

Nowhere in the Big Book does it say you must drink coffee at A.A. meetings. It has become a ritual, however, and, I think, a very destructive one. Coffee, cigarette smoking, and sugar are the three things that I think A.A. as a subculture needs to change. Why? Because caffeine and nicotine are stimulants that lower the quality of recovery. Smoking, of course, also leads to lung cancer and other diseases. Many alcoholics (up to 40 percent) are hypoglycemic and thus are adversely affected by sugar. I strongly suggest that all groups have decaffeinated coffee available and include some sugar-free snacks.

These recommendations have nothing at all to do with the A.A. program. These are social amenities that occur at meetings, but I am convinced that if the founders had known about the adverse health effects of nicotine and caffeine, they would have strongly discouraged smoking and caffeine use at meetings.

After the break, the meeting starts again and individual members make comments or briefly share their personal reactions to the speaker. The goal of most closed meetings is to give everyone present the chance to make a brief comment. Many meetings close with the Lord's Prayer, but some do not. Each group decides this by "group conscience," and individual participation is optional.

Following the meeting, there is "fellowship," which means members go out for refreshments and talk about what happened at the meeting. The fellowship that occurs between meetings is where people begin to rebuild their social skills—people involved in a sober extended family. Twelve Step programs are not just meetings; they are a sober, recovery-focused, social network. And this, together with the Steps and sponsorship, creates a sobriety-oriented community that makes recovery happen.

THE FIRST MEETING

The first A.A. meeting is critical. If newcomers have a positive experience, they probably will come back. If they have a negative one, they may not. As a counselor, I have talked with many people who went to A.A. for the first time and hated it. Most of them unconsciously set themselves up to have a negative experience. Having heard enough of their horror stories over the years, I have developed a guaranteed method for experiencing a terrible first A.A. meeting. If your first meeting is bad, you have a perfect excuse never to go back. Here are the steps you take:

First, find a meeting that is many miles from your home. Why? If you go to a meeting close to home, someone may know you and you don't want any friends or neighbors to know you're an alcoholic.

Second, leave late for the meeting. Figure out how long it will take to get there and subtract four minutes. Rationalize by saying that if you arrive too early, you are going to be hanging around for five or ten minutes with nothing to do. This forces you to drive fast and become anxious.

Third, don't find out the exact location of the meeting; just know it's in the church between 152nd and 153rd streets. When you get there, you'll figure out which of the three churches on the block has the meeting. Don't find out the exact room, either. Discover that there are seven meetings going on at the same time. Open each door and ask, "Is this the Twelve Step meeting?" Above all, don't call the central office of the Twelve Step group you want to attend. If you do, someone might offer to take you to the meeting so you won't get lost or be embarrassed.

Fourth, when you finally find the right meeting, be sure to try to sneak in quietly. If the door hinges squeak loudly as you open the door, smile warmly as everyone turns around and looks at you. Now you have a perfect excuse to sit in the corner feeling embarrassed.

Fifth, as you listen to the people talk, don't just listen— judge. That's very important. Judge others. When you arrive, look over each person in the room and try to guess what psychiatric problem or social deviancy brought him or her here. Pick out the schizophrenics, the child molesters, the criminals, and the rapists. Then "compare out." Say to yourself, Hey, I'm not like any of these people. I don't belong here, I don't fit in. Become very critical. If you agree with something, ignore it. If you disagree with it, remember it so you can tell your therapist about it.

Sixth, isolate yourself. You already arrived late and sat in the corner. During the break, don't talk to anybody, don't introduce yourself to anyone. Don't comment at the meeting and then leave about two minutes before the meeting is over. Then, on your way home, sit in the car and tell yourself, What an unfriendly bunch of people they were! Convince yourself that they really didn't care.

These six guidelines for having a negative first experience may seem absurd, but many newcomers inadvertently do many of these things. The knowledge of what not to do can help people understand what they can do to increase their chances of having a positive first experience.

First, choose a meeting near your home or office that you can reach easily. The easier it is to get there, the more likely it is that you will keep going.

Second, call the central office of the Twelve Step program

you want to attend. Most are listed in the phone book as well as with directory assistance. Mention that you want to go to a meeting and ask if someone could either pick you up or meet you there. That way, before the meeting starts, you will know at least one person who can introduce you to the others.

Third, find out exactly where the meeting is to be sure you don't get lost. Get the exact address and the name or number of the meeting room.

Fourth, get to the meeting at least ten minutes before it is scheduled to start. This gives you time to find the right room, introduce yourself to a few people, and settle in before the meeting begins.

Fifth, walk up to the first three people you see, shake their hands, and say to them, "This is my first meeting and I'd like to get to know some people!" If you do this, you won't be left alone. People will go out of their way to say hello and talk with you.

Sixth, when it's time for you to comment, say, "This is my first meeting, and I'm wondering if any of you would be willing to help me learn a little bit more about the program. I've got time after the meeting to talk, if anyone is willing to help me." You can say anything else you want, but just make sure you say, "This is my first meeting, and I need help in learning about the program."

Seventh, at the end of the meeting, try to connect with several members and go out for coffee. There generally is a group that meets at a specific restaurant after each meeting. Don't be shy. Twelve Step attendees usually are open about inviting newcomers. Over coffee, talk about your reaction to your first meeting.

Eighth, start a recovery journal. Buy a spiral-bound notebook and begin keeping track of your thoughts, feelings, and reactions to the meetings. In your first entry, record the most important things that you heard at the meeting. Make a note of aspects you agreed with or liked. Also make notes of what you did not agree with or like. Remember, you don't have to agree with everything you hear. The goal of Twelve Step meetings is to teach you how to think in a sober way. The goal is not for you to turn off your mind and stop thinking. Just because you hear things you don't like or don't agree with, don't stop going. There is the saying "If two people agree about everything, then at least one of them is unnecessary." Exposing yourself to controversial new ways of thinking about addiction and recovery is a vital first step. Take what fits at that time and leave the rest. Try to keep an open mind and listen.

Take it all back to your next individual or group therapy session—your therapist will want to hear about your reactions. Here's what happened. Here's what I liked; here's what I disliked. Tell your group about it and get their feedback.

When you go to your first meeting, you probably will have a war going on inside your head—the war between your addictive self and your sober self. Your addictive self will try to talk the newcomer out of staying there. Your sober self will fight back, but not very hard.

A typical internal conversation goes like this:

The sober self says, "I think it's a good idea to stay at the meeting."

The addictive self will protest by saying, "This is a dumb meeting! Get out of here! You don't belong here!"

The sober self then says, "I think you should stay; it's not that bad. It's even kind of interesting."

The addictive self argues, "What do you mean you should stay? This is terrible! Look at all these stupid people! You aren't like any of these people!"

Knowing ahead of time that you may have this kind of

inner conflict will help you recognize it when it happens. You can then decide whether to listen to your sober self or your addictive self; you can choose to "compare in" instead of "compare out." You can notice how you are similar to those in the group instead of how you are different. You are also more likely to be receptive, to listen without judging, and to hear what is being said.

4

AN OVERVIEW OF THE TWELVE STEPS

T he heart and soul of A.A. and other Twelve Step programs is the Twelve Steps. Depending on how well they understand and practice the principles contained within these Steps, people recover or stay sick.

The Twelve Steps of A.A. are suggested as a program of recovery, but nobody has to use them. Father Martin once elaborated upon the word *suggested* when he said, "I believe the founders of A.A. suggested that we use the Twelve Steps in the same way that a parachute instructor suggests that we use a parachute when we jump out of an airplane. We don't have to take the suggestion, but there are definite consequences if we don't."

The Steps were written down by Bill Wilson, but Bill did not claim the credit for them. The Steps were developed from the experiences of the early A.A. members as they struggled to recover. The early members shared their experiences, both positive and negative. They carefully noted what worked and then kept it. They also noted what did not work and left that behind. What survived were twelve simple principles that have proved effective for many people.

It is important to note that the Steps are numbered sequentially, which implies that they are to be worked in that order. It is recommended that the First Step be worked thoroughly before going on to the Second Step, and so forth. In A.A., this recommendation is captured in the slogan "First things first." The consequences of not working the Steps in the suggested order are captured in the concept of a "two-stepper"—a person who takes the First Step and then skips a series of other Steps. Many two-steppers relapse because they fail to assemble all of the vital building blocks of recovery.

The Steps are meant to be worked more than once. After working through the Steps a first time, most people typically go back to Step One and start all over again. From their changed perspective in recovery, they learn something new each time they review the Steps. As a result, most members view Twelve Step work as a lifelong process.

The Steps were also meant to be worked on two levels: the conscious and the unconscious. When you work the Steps unconsciously, you intuitively recognize the need for taking the Step as well as the wisdom in the recommended actions. The Step feels right and you know that you need to do it, even though you can't fully explain why. When you work a Step consciously, you think about it and talk it through. You formalize exercises to help yourself get a better conscious understanding of the Step and how it applies to you. When you consciously understand the Step, you can explain what the Step means and why you need it. Some people, for example, experience the reality of powerlessness over alcohol but never think about it. The Step feels right, and by consciously thinking about it, the reality of their alcoholism and the need for sobriety become obvious. For others, conscious understanding comes first. They think and talk about the issue of loss of control, consciously examine their drinking history and life problems, and decide they are out of control. Then their unconscious catches up as they become comfortable on a deep gut level with the reality of their alcoholism and their need for abstinence.

In this chapter, I will present a brief summary of the Twelve Steps. The goal is to show you the big picture of what the Steps are and where they are going. In subsequent chapters, I will review each Step in greater detail.

THE TWELVE STEPS OF A.A.

Step One
We admitted we were powerless over alcohol—that our lives had become unmanageable.

In the First Step, you admit that you cannot control your drinking or drug use and because of that powerlessness, your life is out of control. The First Step is designed to help alcoholics grasp a basic and undeniable fact: Whenever you use alcohol (or other drugs), you can never be sure what is going to happen. This is the essence of being out of control. Sometimes alcoholics drink in moderation with no adverse affects. At other times, without any rhyme or reason, their drinking escalates and they act out in ways that hurt both themselves and those they love.

These episodes of loss of control make their lives unmanageable and cause them to feel shame, guilt, and nagging pain. They try to stop but can't. So they try again and fail again. With each new failure, their shame, guilt, and pain increase. Their shame and guilt cause denial. They lie to themselves about what is happening and they try to lie to others. They have tried everything they know how to try and nothing has worked. They have lost hope. They realize that they can't do it alone using the old ways of thinking, but they know of no other way. In A.A. terms, they have hit bottom. The booze has defeated them, and they are ready to stop trying to be normal drinkers and do something else.

The First Step has been adapted for use in other Twelve Step programs. For example, the First Step of Narcotics Anonymous reads: "We admitted that we were powerless over our addiction, that our lives have become unmanageable." The first step of ACoA reads: "We admitted that we were powerless over the effects of alcoholism and our lives had become unmanageable."

The key to working a First Step is to recognize that you have a problem, then acknowledge that you have tried everything that you know to solve the problem and none of it worked. In essence, you honestly acknowledge that you can't solve this problem by doing the things that you have learned how to do. In short—"You can't do it alone."

Step Two
Came to believe that a Power greater than ourselves could restore us to sanity.

In Step Two, you become open to the possibility that there is someone or something out there that is able to provide a way to help you solve your problems. This Step asks you to believe that someone or something more powerful than you can help you stop drinking or drugging. You are asked to believe that there is someone or something smarter, stronger, and more knowledgeable than you—that there is a way out.

At the core of the Second Step is the belief in some kind of a Higher Power that can help you. You need to believe that there is a frame of reference that is larger than your own addictive mentality; that it is possible to understand what has happened to you and to learn what you need to do in order to recover. And, most important, you need to believe that you can tap into a source of courage, strength, and hope that will allow you to cope. After completing the Second Step, you can say with complete honesty, "We can't, but somebody else can." You don't have to know what or who that Higher Power is; you just have to believe that it exists and become willing to search for it.

Step Three
Made a decision to turn our will and our lives over to the care of God *as we understood Him.*

Step Three tells recovering people to trust in a Higher Power. In other words, find some expert advice and follow it. They must become willing to take direction from their newfound Higher Power and see what happens.

But who or what is the Higher Power? A.A. states very clearly that it is up to you to find your own Higher Power. Notice that the terms *Higher Power* and *God* are used interchangeably. A.A. does not prescribe a specific concept of God, but rather instructs its members to find a God of their own understanding.

In my understanding, the Higher Power serves two functions. The first is emotional—it gives people the courage, strength, and hope to move ahead in recovery. The second is intellectual and behavioral—it gives them the knowledge about what they need to do and then motivates them to do it. If they have chosen their Higher Power correctly, when they connect with it, they will become motivated to learn what they need to do to recover. When they do it, it works, and when it works, they will become encouraged to do more.

You can select God as your Higher Power, but many members, especially new members, do not. They use their Twelve Step group as their initial Higher Power. The group meets all of the criteria. By going to meetings and talking honestly with group members, you can tap into a strong belief that recovery is possible. You can develop the courage, strength, and hope to go on. By listening to the stories of your group members, you can learn what to do in order to get well. As you work at your recovery, you can share your progress and problems with other people who will listen to you, understand your struggles, and take seriously what you are saying.

In Step One you said, "I can't!" In Step Two you said, "Somebody else can!" Now, in Step Three you say, "I'm going to let them!"

Step Four
Made a searching and fearless moral inventory of ourselves.

After working the first three Steps, you are into the program. You are willing to accept and follow advice. The first definitive piece of advice you receive is in Step Four, which tells you to examine yourself critically to find out who you really are. You need to look within and inventory your strengths and weaknesses so you can build on your strengths and overcome your weaknesses. It is only through an honest knowledge of yourself and your motivations that you can find long-term sobriety. You must be willing to challenge the misperceptions and mistaken beliefs that you hold. Even if it hurts, you must get to know who you really are in both your strengths and your weaknesses. This rigorous honesty forms the foundation of recovery.

Step Five
Admitted to God, to ourselves, and to another human being the exact nature of our wrongs.

In Step Five, you need to admit both your addiction and the character defects you found in Step Four that drive you back into your old addictive ways of coping. You are instructed to (1) admit to yourself; (2) affirm with your Higher Power; and then (3) share with another person, as honestly as you are able, your inventory of your strengths and weaknesses. This inventory is not a litany of sins, but rather an honest evaluation of what you have learned about yourself and your self-defeating behaviors.

In A.A., this is humility. And it doesn't mean you put yourself down. Humility means you know who you are, know where you are coming from, and accept that it's okay for you to have your particular strengths and weaknesses.

It is only by confronting yourself in a dialogue with another human being that you can truly come to terms with what has happened to you and who you have become as a result of your addictive experiences. Sharing painful past memories with another, caring person—one who will understand what you are saying, take you seriously, and affirm your experiences as real and valid—provides a sense of relief. You no longer feel alone. You no longer feel like an outcast. You realize that others have done things similar to what you have done. You can see that you belong and can recover.

Step Six
Were entirely ready to have God remove all these defects of character.

By working Step Six, you live with a conscious awareness of the character defects that you discovered in Steps Four and Five. By being constantly aware of your character defects and the pain they are causing you and those you love, you become ready and willing to give them up. You keep asking for the courage, the strength, and the means whereby you can correct them.

Step Seven
Humbly asked Him to remove our shortcomings.

In Step Seven, you ask your Higher Power to remove your shortcomings. You ask for the strength to do what you need to do to change and grow and leave your addictive self behind. Your Higher Power gives you the courage and strength to give up your character defects, but you must do the actual giving-up. You must take action and do what A.A. calls "the legwork." A.A. literature constantly points out this dual role—turning to a Higher Power for courage, strength, and hope, and then putting this newfound strength into action. A.A. members often say it very clearly: "Pray for potatoes but be willing to pick up a hoe!"

Asking for the removal of your defects facilitates an internal change that prepares you for Steps Eight and Nine. You repair yourself inwardly so you can begin repairing your life outwardly. The healing process moves from the inside to the outside. First you change what you think and feel, then you can change how you act. Next you can repair the damage you did to others through your addiction.

Step Eight
Made a list of all persons we had harmed, and became willing to make amends to them all.

In Step Eight, you come to the realization that your past addictive behavior damaged other people. You make a list of those people and recognize that you must make an honest attempt to repair the hurt you did to them. In other words, you acknowledge that you must make amends.

Step Nine
Made direct amends to such people wherever possible, except when to do so would injure them or others.

You make amends to all you have harmed. You actually repair any damage you have caused, wherever or whenever it is in your power to do so. You "clean house" and make room for spiritual growth.

Step Ten
Continued to take personal inventory and when we
were wrong promptly admitted it.

You take inventory of yourself daily, examining your
thoughts, feelings, and actions. When you goof, when you
create a problem, when you prove you are a fallible human
being, you fix the problems as quickly as you can and to the
best of your abilities. This frees you to make your primary
focus that of spiritual growth in your recovery.

Step Eleven
Sought through prayer and meditation to improve our
conscious contact with God *as we understood Him,*
praying only for knowledge of His will for us and the
power to carry that out.

While practicing your addiction, alcohol and drugs distorted your spiritual values. By *spiritual,* I mean the nonphysical aspect of your being—your thoughts, feelings,
attitudes, and values. As you clear the wreckage from the
past, you can at last experience a new sense of spiritual
freedom. You can contact the psychic energy or life force
within you in new and exciting ways. You can learn to
become still and listen to that quiet, yet powerful voice
within you that connects you to your true values in life. In
A.A. terms, you can develop conscious contact with the
God of your understanding—your Higher Power.

Step Twelve

Having had a spiritual awakening as the result of these Steps, we tried to carry this message to alcoholics, and to practice these principles in all our affairs.

What A.A. calls a "spiritual awakening" is a radical transformation or change in perception, attitude, and personality. You begin to feel changed because you are thinking differently, managing your feelings differently, and acting differently. You have changed in subtle yet profound ways. Because of these changes, you are ready to go out and carry the message of what you have learned and experienced to other recovering people. It is important to remember that Step Twelve also instructs you to keep practicing Twelve Step principles in all of your affairs. Thus, working the Twelve Step program never really ends.

Those are the Twelve Steps in a nutshell. This overview provides a shorthand version for understanding the Steps. The principles that underlie each of the Steps are explored in detail in chapters 5 through 16. Following the material on each Step is a checklist that summarizes the tasks and objectives of the Step presented in that chapter. This checklist is designed to be used as a self-assessment tool to help evaluate how thoroughly you have worked each Step.

5

I CAN'T

The essence of the First Step is to admit that you cannot control your addiction and that your addiction is making it impossible to manage your life. In order to do this, you have to understand clearly that drinking and drugging are the causes of many of your problems. This is tough, because many alcoholics would like to believe that their problems cause them to drink, and that if they could just get a handle on their problems, their drinking would magically stop being a problem. The purpose of the First Step is to help you see the true cause-and-effect relationship between drinking and drugging and life problems. For chemical addicts, drinking and drugging cause life problems. To solve these problems, they must first stop drinking and drugging. There are four aspects of this Step with which you must come to terms in order to understand it at a deep level.

1. You admit that alcohol and drug use has caused major life problems.

The operational word is *admit*, meaning, "You consciously acknowledge, or become aware, that your alcohol and drug use causes problems." You have to acknowledge that once you put alcohol in your system, you can no longer control what you are going to do next. Once you start drinking, you can't guarantee when or if you will stop or what you will or won't do.

Father Martin says it very clearly: "To solve a problem, you first have to admit you have a problem. And what causes a problem is a problem." The key here is that if drinking causes you problems, then you have a drinking problem. If you evade that point and try to deal with the secondary issues that surround drinking, you are not going to get well.

The process of taking a First Step means you have to think clearly, logically, and rationally about your alcohol- and drug-using behavior. You have to understand the cause-and-effect sequence related to your drinking behavior and your life problems.

Clear thinking means you are able to tell others what you think. Most chemically dependent people don't think about their drinking and drug use. They have trained themselves to avoid thinking about it. This process is called denial.

The First Step also invites you to think logically. This means you don't contradict yourself and you don't go to war with yourself when thinking about or talking about your drinking and drug use.

At this stage of recovery, when most chemically dependent people start thinking about alcohol and drug use, a battle erupts in their heads. The addictive self pops out and says, "Don't think about this," and the sober self says, "You had better think about it because it's killing you!" There is an internal dissonance, an internal battle that emerges between the addictive self and the sober self.

To work the First Step, you also have to think rationally. Your inner logic system must correspond to external reality. When you're thinking clearly about your chemical use, you can tell others: (1) how much alcohol and drugs you use; (2) how often you use them; (3) what you want to accomplish by your use; and (4) what the actual consequences of your use have been. These are the first four questions you want to explore in taking a First Step—How much? How often? What for? and What consequences?

To answer these questions, you have to think clearly, and that is not as easy as it sounds. When recovering people begin to sort out their thinking, most of them come up with alibis, excuses, self-deceptions, and outright lies. Their thinking about their drinking generally is irrational.

Let's look at how one alcoholic named Sam viewed his drinking. Sam was referred to me for alcoholism counseling after being arrested for driving while intoxicated. When I asked Sam how often he drank, he said, "Not very often at all." When I asked him, "How often is not very often?" he told me that he drank something every day. (Notice the addictive thinking: "Not very often" means "I do it every day.")

When I asked Sam if he had ever gotten drunk, he emphatically said, "No!" Since Sam was arrested for driving while intoxicated, I became confused. "Excuse me, Sam," I said, scratching my head. "If you have never been drunk, how could you have gotten arrested for driving while intoxicated? What was your blood alcohol level when you were arrested?"

"They told me it was 0.2, but I think they're wrong," he

rationalized. "I know when I'm drunk and when I'm not. And I wasn't drunk!"

"How do you know if you're drunk?"

"I'm drunk when I drink so much that I'm unconscious —that's drunk. As long as I'm awake and functioning, I'm not drunk and the cops should leave me alone."

Not being discouraged easily, I asked if he had ever had any problems because of his drinking.

"No!"

"Are you sure?"

"Absolutely! Drinking doesn't cause any problems in my life!"

"Are you married?"

"Not anymore."

"Why not?"

"My wife divorced me."

"Why did she divorce you?"

"She said she couldn't stand my drinking."

"But I thought you said you had no problems because of your drinking."

"I don't," Sam snapped. "She really left me because I didn't make enough money for her rich tastes. My drinking was just the excuse that she used!"

Most alcoholics have strange ways of defining problems. Perhaps you have seen those T-shirts that say, "I don't have a drinking problem. I drink. I get drunk. I fall down. No problem!" This is the kind of reasoning most alcoholics use. "I don't have a drinking or drug problem. I drink. I get drunk. I get divorced. I get fired. I kill innocent people by driving drunk. I go to jail for two years. No problem!"

This is what denial is all about—self-deception at its best. Alcoholics know that they are not addicted, and to prove it, they define addiction in such a way that they are sure not to have it! One major goal in taking the First Step is to interrupt denial and begin to think clearly and accurately about your drinking and drug use and its consequences.

When you dig into the First Step, it often starts to get confusing. You find inconsistencies and self-deceptions. As you challenge these mistaken beliefs, powerful memories and feelings can well up within you.

What are the real consequences of alcohol and drug use? Do you do things when you drink that you would not do if you didn't drink? Are you consciously aware that using alcohol and drugs is causing problems? Alcoholics defend themselves with a wall of denial. So, in working the First Step, you must come to see that alcohol and drug use is causing the problems. You have to understand clearly the cause-and-effect relationship between chemical use and life problems.

One of the biggest obstacles to taking the First Step is that alcoholics often don't know what the truth is. They have lied to themselves so many times that they have come to believe their own lies. They are sincerely deluded. If you took most actively drinking alcoholics and hooked them up to a lie detector, then asked them if they thought they were alcoholics, many would answer no, and the lie detector would show that they were telling the truth. Why? Because they sincerely do not believe they are alcoholics. What do they usually believe instead? Many believe that they have life problems that are causing them to drink, and if they could solve those problems, their drinking problems would be over. In order to work the First Step, this inverted cause-and-effect relationship has to be challenged.

So the first task in working Step One is to challenge this inverted cause-and-effect relationship by asking these questions: Is it really true? Where is the evidence that supports it? Is there another way to think about it?

Let's see how this works. Al came into alcoholism counseling when his wife threatened to divorce him because of his drinking. Al was convinced that his marital problems caused him to drink. When I asked him to tell me about the marital problems, he said, "She won't have sex with me; that's why I get drunk." When I asked why she wouldn't have sex with him, he claimed that he didn't know. I asked him to tell me about the last time he had asked his wife for sex and she had refused.

"I came home at night and I wanted to have sex with her, and she wouldn't."

"What time was it?"

"It was three-thirty or four in the morning."

"Had you been drinking?"

"Yes, but I wasn't drunk, just mellow. You know what I mean. I was feeling high and real sexy."

Then Al told me the whole story. He arrived home, went into the bedroom, turned on the light, and woke up his wife. "I want to have sex," he said, as he pushed his way into bed. His wife refused, they had an argument, and she threw him out of the bedroom to spend the night on the couch! His wife refused to talk with him for a week.

"Did this have anything to do with your drinking?" I asked.

"No. The problem is that I've got a frigid wife!"

This is the type of reasoning that alcoholics use before they have taken a good First Step. "If my wife doesn't want to have sex with me when I'm drunk, that means she's frigid." To overcome these types of rationalizations, individuals have to learn how to relate cause and effect. In this case, I asked Al, "Have you ever asked your wife to have sex with you when you were sober?" Al said he had.

"And what did she say?"

"She said yes."

"That's very interesting," I said. "When you're sober,

48

she has sex with you. When you are drunk, she doesn't. Could there be a relationship here?"

A confused look came over Al's face. After a few moments, he said, "Maybe my drinking does have something to do with it."

Another example of this distorted cause-and-effect relationship was provided by a woman named Sue, who was referred to me by her employer for evaluation of the cause of her excessive tardiness and absenteeism. When I asked Sue what she thought the problem was, she replied, "My boss is irrational! He wants to fire me!" When I asked her to explain why, Sue told me.

"He says I'm late in the morning." When I asked Sue if this was true, she said yes. Then I asked her if her tardiness had anything to do with drinking.

"Absolutely not!" she said emphatically, with a hurt look on her face.

"What days do you usually come in late?"

"Monday mornings."

"What do you usually do on Sunday nights?"

"I usually drink a lot."

"Are you ever hung over on Mondays?"

"Well, yes."

"Do your hangovers have anything to do with your being late or absent?"

"Well, you can't expect me to go to work if I'm sick, can you? I think my boss is lucky that I get there at all, considering the way I feel some Monday mornings!"

Finally Sue had begun to connect her drinking with her work problems.

This is First Step work. It may seem simplistic, but at this stage of recovery, chemically dependent people need help in seeing the cause-and-effect relationship between their chemical use and other problems. One alcoholism counselor calls these basic insights "blinding flashes of the obvious."

One way to take a First Step is to make a list of your problems and then ask, "How is alcohol involved?" When people first get sober, they usually find that most of their problems have been connected in some way to their drinking and drugging. In some cases, such as being too sick to go to work, the alcohol and drug use directly causes the problem. In other cases, legitimate life problems are made worse when they try to handle them by drinking and drugging. They can end up getting trapped in a cycle of addiction. They have problems that cause drinking and drugging, the drinking and drugging causes more problems, which result in more drinking and drugging, and so on. When they take the First Step, they see this cycle clearly and come to believe on a deep level that drinking and drugging cannot work as a solution to these problems.

Once you know that alcohol and drug use is causing your problems, you are ready to move on to the second task of the First Step.

2. You admit that you are powerless to control the use of alcohol or drugs.

When alcoholics put alcohol or other mood-altering drugs in their bodies, they can no longer predict what they are going to do. This reaction is not governed by any complex psychological law; it's governed by basic physiology. When the chemically dependent person begins to drink, brain chemistry is altered and judgment goes out the window. A biopsychosocial craving is set up that results in loss of control.

Not everyone who drinks alcohol loses control over their drinking. Alcoholics do because they have a genetic predisposition to be alcoholic, and other people don't. If you have a genetic predisposition to become alcoholic, you're physiologically programmed to lose control over your drinking and drug use. You cannot predict what you are going to do as a result.

Chemically dependent people don't turn into raving maniacs every time they drink, but once they start drinking, they can never be sure of what is going to happen. Sometimes they drink a little and then quit. At other times, they will keep drinking until they are drunk. They never know for sure whether or not they are going to be able to stop. They suffer from "loss of control."

At first they're in total control. They rarely if ever get drunk, and if they do have a hangover, it's very mild. Then they begin to get drunk accidentally. It happens occasionally at first and then with greater frequency. It is only in the late, terminal stages of the disease that a person loses control every time he or she drinks.

Can alcoholics learn to control their drinking? A.A. members, who have researched this question extensively by personal experimentation, say no. And this opinion is endorsed strongly by most major authorities. If you are alcoholic, you need to abstain totally if you are to recover.

3. You admit that your life has become unmanageable as a result of alcohol or drug use.

What does "unmanageable" mean? It means you have problems that are interfering with your ability to live the way you want to live. In other words, it means that you have lost control of your life. There are problems going on in your life that you can't solve. Since these problems are caused by your use of alcohol and drugs, you will never be able to solve them until you stop putting alcohol and drugs into your body.

51

4. You admit you are powerless to manage your own life effectively as long as you continue to use alcohol or drugs.
The fourth task in the First Step is to recognize that your old problems will return if you start using alcohol and drugs again. The disease is called alcoholism, not "alcohol-wasm." Just because you are abstinent does not mean the disease goes away. I have seen the tragedy of alcoholics who have been sober for as long as eighteen years and have made the mistake of thinking they could handle it. The devastation is usually total, complete, and extremely fast.

Once you lose control over drinking and drugging, the ability to control will never come back. Your only alternative is to learn how to live life as a sober human being by coping with your day-to-day problems with the help of others.

So, what does it take to work the First Step thoroughly?

If you are fully aware of the relationship between alcohol and drugs and the problems that chemical use has caused in your life, you have completed that part of the First Step. If you are not firmly convinced that alcohol and drugs have caused the bulk of your life problems, task one of the First Step is only partially completed. If you have never thought about it, you have not completed this task at all.

If you admit that you are powerless to control the use of alcohol and drugs, if you are consciously aware and fully believe that when you use alcohol or drugs you cannot predict what's going to happen, then you have worked the next task of the First Step fully. If you still doubt this or if you don't believe it, then you have completed this task only partially or not at all.

When you have completed all four of these tasks, what decision do you have to make? What's the only rational decision left? You're alcoholic. And what do you have to do to get well? You have to stop drinking. If you believe these four things, the only rational position to take is that you have to stop. At this point, you are ready to try seriously to stop drinking.

It is important to remember that you work the Steps on the conscious and unconscious levels. Some people experience the reality of powerlessness and life unmanageability before they ever consciously think about it. Other people consciously think about it before they are able to experience or internalize it.

A Step is not worked completely until the head and the gut match. If you say, "I am powerless" and World War III goes off in your head or your gut ties up in a knot, it's not over. You've got more work to do on that Step. Psychologically, this process is called "integration"; understanding alone is not enough. You need emotional acceptance.

"Acting as if" is a start, but it is not enough. There is a big difference between compliance—"Okay, I won't drink for a while"—and surrender—"I know in the core of my being that alcohol and drug use will kill me. If I drink at any time in any way, it's going to create serious problems for me— for my health, for my life, and for the people I love." The First Step isn't complete until the head and the heart match.

At the end of the First Step, you need to become abstinent. For many newcomers, abstinence is kept very simple: It means don't use alcohol or other drugs. As many people progress in the program, they find that their definition of abstinence becomes more expansive.

Abstinence can be viewed as the refusal of drink and drugs and the refusal to do anything that puts you in the immediate risk of drinking and drugging. "I used to believe 'abstinent' just meant don't drink," said a recovering alcoholic named Glen. "Then I had my first relapse and realized that abstinence also means don't hang around with people who are drinking and drugging. When I started hanging around with sober people, it didn't take me very long to realize that even though I wasn't drinking or drugging, I was still thinking and acting like a drunk. So I expanded my definition of abstinence to include not thinking addictive thoughts or acting out with old behaviors I used to use when drinking and drugging."

Abstinence can be viewed as a positive or a negative. Most newly sober people feel it's awful not to be able to drink and drug, but with sober time, they learn that abstinence is the most positive thing in the world. With abstinence comes recovery and with recovery comes health— and life and love. With recovery comes the ability to choose, to learn, and to grow. With recovery comes the opportunity to become truly human again.

Taking a First Step forces you to change how you think, how you manage your feelings, and how you act. I call these three functions TFAs—thoughts, feelings, and actions. You have to interrupt your denial and start regarding your alcohol and drug use as what it really is—a fatal disease that will destroy your life and eventually kill you. You have to learn how to manage your feelings by talking about them instead of medicating them with booze and drugs. You have to learn how to act responsibly and to solve problems as they come up.

Some people change their thinking first, then their behavior, and then their gut follows. Others change their thinking first, and as a result their feelings change, and then they can change their behavior.

Some change their actions first. They stop drinking and start doing things differently. Their new behaviors force them to think differently and to change their feelings. But at some point, all three functions—thinking, feeling, and acting—have to line up.

In the First Step, chemically dependent people must recognize the effect that alcohol and drugs have on them and their individual powerlessness to change or control or stop that effect. THEY can't control alcohol. THEY can't manage their lives. THEY can't handle it. THEY don't know what to do. Alcohol is handling them; they're not handling alcohol. In short, THEY can't.

Then their feelings change. They lose the desire to drink and start wanting to be sober. Finally, they become willing to do whatever is necessary to stop and stay stopped. That's what THEY believe Step One is all about.

POINTS TO REMEMBER

In completing Step One you:

1. Admit that the use of alcohol or drugs has caused major problems in your life.
2. Admit that you are powerless to control the use of alcohol or drugs.
3. Admit that your life has become unmanageable as a result of alcohol or drug use.
4. Admit that you are powerless to manage your life effectively as long as you continue to use alcohol or drugs.

6

SOMEBODY ELSE CAN

Step Two does not say, "... a Power greater than ourselves *did* restore us to sanity." It says, "Came to believe" that one *could*. In Step Two, recovering people develop a sense of faith that there is someone or something bigger and more powerful than they are. There is someone or something out there that knows more about addiction and about recovery than they do. There is someone or something out there that has the answer—someone who can help them get well.

Some people claim that a Higher Power can be anything, even an inanimate object. I know many people who believe it is better to make an empty bottle your Higher Power than it is to have no Higher Power at all. But if you are seriously interested in recovery, it is important to explore carefully the concept of Higher Power to determine its meaning. The word *Higher* means something that is greater, stronger, more knowledgeable, or more capable than you are. The word *Power* means that this something has the energy or ability to act *upon* you or *with* you to promote recovery. There is a big difference between seeking help from an empty bottle, which has no inherent power to help you, and seeking help from a group of recovering alcoholics who do.

Since recovering people use many different definitions of Higher Power, you need a way to organize and make sense out of your options. I use a system that defines the real power to help. At level one, the weakest possible Higher Power, you have inanimate objects that you believe have power but in reality don't. You can pray to a Coca-Cola bottle, but I sincerely doubt that the bottle will answer your prayers. The second level involves another human being who is more knowledgeable about recovery than you are. The third level involves a group of such people working in harmony with you to recover. Finally, there is a supernatural Higher Power that many people choose to call God. This Higher Power is sometimes conceptualized as a personal, loving, and caring God with whom you can communicate.

When people start talking about a Higher Power, I encourage them, at the very least, to rely on someone who is more knowledgeable in the recovery process—and preferably a group of individuals. In my experience, the first Higher Power for the majority of recovering people is the power of their recovery group. It's the power of the group conscience—the collective energy and help available from that group.

Once you believe in a Higher Power, you come to believe that this Higher Power can restore you to sanity. And if you need to be restored to sanity, what are you? You're insane. An "addictive" form of insanity is lurking within you. There is an addictive self that's crazy, that has taken control of your life. So your way to get well is to rely on a Higher

Power, something outside of yourself that's greater than you are and that knows more, that can teach you about recovery and give you more strength, energy, and power than you have individually.

Therefore, the first task of Step Two is to recognize the nature of the insanity of your addiction.

1. You admit that you are suffering from an "addiction-induced insanity" that creates the obsession and compulsion to use alcohol and other drugs.

What is meant by "addiction-induced insanity"? It means using addictive thinking that operates at several levels. The first level is called "euphoric recall." The alcoholic remembers and exaggerates all the good times associated with past drinking and drugging and blocks out all of the bad times associated with it. People in early recovery refer to this as the memories of "the good old days."

Once you have told your story several times, you begin to realize that "the good old days" were not all that good. Once the euphoric recall breaks, you realize that the only good point of alcohol and drug use is the artificial state of euphoria it produced. There's nothing else "good" about it.

Once you recognize that the only things that drugs change are your feelings, you begin to realize that every other benefit you had during your drinking and drugging days could have been had without the booze or drugs. Most of the problems you experienced were either caused or complicated by the drinking and drug use. The only "good" thing you gained from drinking was that it made you feel euphoric. It gave you a temporary sense of well-being.

Euphoric recall leads to positive expectancy. People believe that if only they could drink or drug, everything would be okay. They still tend to believe that alcohol and drugs have the power to fix them. "Boy, if I could only drink in the right way in the future, if I could only drink like a normal person, my life would be magically fixed!"

A typical attitude in early recovery is, "Oh, I know I can't drink, but I'm really being ripped off! Not being able to drink means I can never be happy, I can never have fun, I can never again relax. I know this is killing me, but I'm so miserable because I can't use it anymore!"

Euphoric recall leads to obsession. People in recovery start thinking about how good they felt when they used alcohol and drugs, and they exaggerate the memory of those good times. They also think about how miserable it is to be sober and how great it would be if they could be social drinkers. "If God could give me the biggest miracle in the world, it would be to create a drug that would let me drink like a social drinker!"

The same phenomenon is true for food in Overeaters Anonymous. Do people *without* eating disorders remember how wonderful it was to eat, and do they think about it constantly? Do they look forward with anticipation to their next meal? Do they view food as a way to make them better people? No, they don't. These behaviors are hallmarks of an eating disorder that, though not a chemical dependency, is also based on addiction-induced insanity. People without eating disorders don't think, "If only I could eat like a normal person, then everything would be fine." That's what is meant by addiction-induced insanity.

Simply acknowledging this insanity is not enough. You have to believe that there is someone or something that can help you deal with it.

2. You came to believe that this addiction-induced insanity could only be removed with outside help.

Addictive insanity is marked by three major symptoms. First, you expect different outcomes from the same behavior. When you get sober, you want to continue to cope with life just as you have always done. When it doesn't work, you just dig in and try the same daily methods over and over again.

Jake is an example of this. When drinking, he could always scare his wife into doing what he wanted her to do. When he got sober, he refused to change this. When he wanted his wife to do something, he would yell, scream, and intimidate her. After a year of sobriety, he was shocked when his wife divorced him.

The second symptom is self-centeredness that prevents you from noticing other people. As a result, many recovering people genuinely don't believe there is anyone out there who is willing or able to help them.

The third symptom of addictive insanity is grandiosity. You believe that you are smarter and more important than anyone else. As a result, you often are unwilling to believe that anyone outside of yourself can help you.

Once you understand that you have this addiction-induced insanity, you have to come to believe that there is a way out. The way out starts by not drinking and drugging, but there is far more to it than that. Not drinking—what A.A. calls abstinence—is only the ticket to get into the movie house. It's not the show. Did you ever stand in line for a long time on a cold night to get into a movie, finally get your ticket, and then say, "Now that I've got the ticket, I'm going to go home"? That's what many chemically dependent people do when they stop drinking without working the program.

In A.A., abstinence is viewed as a necessary first step to recovery. It isn't recovery. Recovery is overcoming your addiction-induced insanity by working the Steps and going to any lengths to change yourself into the kind of person who no longer needs to drink or drug.

3. You admit that you have attitudes, beliefs, and rationalizations that prevent you from accepting outside help.

What attitudes? "I believe I'm better than everybody else. There's nobody good enough to help me." What beliefs? "I've got to depend on myself. If I ever let anyone else try to help me, the world is going to crumble under my feet." What rationalizations? "It's not my fault I'm this way," or "In this world, my way is the sane way to be."

Alcoholics have to acknowledge that they have attitudes, beliefs, and rationalizations that prevent them from asking for or accepting the help that they need. These things also block their ability to receive help.

4. You develop the belief that there is a Power greater than yourself that can remove your obsession to use alcohol and other drugs.

There is something greater than yourself that can remove these blocks. Now that you're not drinking, when you're abstinent, the obsession and the compulsion are still there. There are times when you want to drink and drug. At times the urge can take the form of overpowering obsessions and compulsions that you can't manage alone. You need help, but shame and guilt often block you from reaching out and asking for the help you need.

The basic problem is that you can't get out of yourself. You need to turn to a Higher Power but feel unable to do so. You need some source of courage, inspiration, and strength that's bigger than you are to help you get through these periods. At this stage, I recommend a spiritual Higher Power plus what I call a "substitute Higher Power," which is other people. You need both.

Your spiritual Higher Power gives a source of courage, strength, and hope that allows you to stay sober and do what you need to do to get well. Other people provide you with practical know-how and immediate support to guide you through the crisis.

Chemical dependence is a disease of hopelessness. Just as mold grows in darkness, chemical addictions grow in despair. To recover, you must make a leap of faith. You must come to believe that you can get well. How do you do that? The formula is simple, but it isn't easy. You make a decision that you will no longer tolerate your life the way it is. In A.A. terms, you "hit bottom" and say, "Enough is enough; I'm sick and tired of being sick and tired!"

The leap of faith is often triggered by pain. In essence, many people in recovery are jolted sober by the painful reality of their addiction. In the film *Butch Cassidy and the Sundance Kid*, both Butch and Sundance are trapped on a high cliff by a posse. They know that if they stay there, they will be killed. The only way out is to jump off the cliff into a river rapids below. Butch turns to Sundance and says, "Let's jump!" Sundance says, "I can't! I don't know how to swim!" Butch looks at him, laughs, and says, "Don't worry about that—the jump will probably kill us anyway." This is the leap of faith. I don't know how to stop drinking and drugging, a part of me doesn't want to stop, but I'm going to do it anyway because I've had enough. I refuse to keep living in my addiction.

When taking a leap of faith, you have to jump into a recovery environment. That means getting to meetings, talking to sober people, reading recovery-oriented literature, and working the Steps. If your leap of faith in recovery takes you to a bar or the home of a drinking buddy, the faith in recovery will dissolve quickly.

Recovery is a miracle, but the miracle isn't magic. The miracle happens because you are willing to put simple principles to work in your recovery. Faith is born when you can see clearly that drinking and drugging is causing severe problems, that these problems will keep getting worse, and that there is a way out. The faith is actualized when you leap into a recovery program and start going to meetings and working the Steps with a sponsor. The faith is solidified when you see that it works, when you begin to be freed from the obsession and compulsion to use alcohol and other drugs.

5. You search for a Power outside of yourself that can help you to recover from addiction.

This is Second Step work. You have to start looking for this power and you don't even know what it is. You start to search. You begin a journey, a process of trying to find a way out of your insanity.

For most people, their sponsor and their recovery group help show them the way to an understanding of a spiritual Higher Power and give them a source of courage, strength, and hope on which they can draw.

6. You find a Power greater than yourself that is capable of removing the obsession and compulsion to use alcohol and other drugs.

And this Higher Power is capable of removing the denial and obsession that block you from using that source of help to restore you to sanity. And what is this process, this Power that can remove your alcohol-induced insanity?

In Step One, we defined abstinence in a negative sense. Abstinence also has a positive side to it. Psychological theory tells us that if you try to break a habit by stopping it without replacing it with something else, the habit comes back. You have to stop practicing one habit and then develop a substitute habit to replace it. The substitute habit, which is healthier, often is called a "positive addiction"—a positive dependency or compulsion. It is something to do that is healthier than the self-destructive behavior it replaces.

In A.A., people are encouraged to give up their dependence on alcohol and other drugs and learn to rely upon spirituality to generate the positive mental, emotional, and spiritual states of mind called "serenity." In A.A., they are taught to replace the escape of addictive highs with the serenity and peace of mind that come from living a sober and responsible life. There is true satisfaction in developing meaningful values, making a commitment to live in accordance with those values whenever possible, and then doing it. They find these values by practicing principles of absolute truthfulness.

So, in the negative sense, A.A. says, "Stop thinking and acting like a drunk or a druggie, don't use alcohol or other drugs, and avoid people, places, and things that may lead back to drug use." So what are you to do instead? A.A. tells you to practice a program of rigorous honesty and to begin changing how you think, how you manage your feelings, and what you do. How to do this? By taking a leap of faith that involves going to meetings, getting a sponsor, working the Steps, living the sober life, and associating with sober people. Put the program to the test. Try it and see if it works. Remember, there is a guarantee. If you don't like the experience of being sober, you can go back to drinking and drugging and get double your misery back.

Many chemically dependent people stop drinking and then continue to think, act, feel, and relate to others as if they were still drinking. This is called a "dry drunk." People who stop drinking and drugging and don't change anything are often miserable in sobriety. Susan is an example of this. When drinking, Susan was very isolated and self-centered. She always drank alone and avoided other people. She felt superior to others and privately criticized everyone she met. No one was good enough to be her friend, so she stayed home alone and drank. When her drinking went out of control and she ended up in detox, she decided to stop drinking. She attended meetings but judged everyone she met. She didn't meet one person in the program whom she considered likable. She refused to get a sponsor or to study A.A. literature, and she was miserable. Although not drinking, she was continuing to think, feel, and act out in the same way that she did when she was drinking.

When Susan started counseling because she felt like killing herself, she told me her problem very clearly: "I like the way I am! I don't want to change! Why can't I just keep thinking and acting the way I always have? I'm not drinking, but why should I have to change?"

In the positive aspect, recovery means change. It means learning new ways of thinking and managing your feelings. It means learning new ways of acting and responding to others. In recovery you learn how to think clearly, logically, and rationally. You also learn to recognize and talk about your feelings. Most important, you learn how to act responsibly and how to relate to others in healthy, constructive ways. You stop recycling old behaviors that don't work and learn more effective ways of coping with life's problems.

This is what the program is about—changing on a variety of levels. When you do it long enough, you begin to know intuitively how to do it. Your spiritual self takes over because you are now in the habit of responsible living. You have peace of mind because you no longer have to force yourself to act responsibly. You *are* responsible.

In psychological terms, you have integrated a new self-concept, and this takes time and faith. In completing Step Two, you demonstrate faith that recovery is possible.

POINTS TO REMEMBER

In completing Step Two you:

1. Come to believe that you are suffering from an "addiction-induced insanity" that creates the obsession and compulsion to use alcohol and other drugs.
2. Come to believe that your addiction-induced insanity can only be removed with outside help.
3. Come to believe that you have developed attitudes, beliefs, and rationalizations that prevent you from accepting outside help.
4. Come to believe that there is a Power greater than yourself that can remove your obsession to use alcohol and other drugs.
5. Come to believe that you need to search for a Power outside of yourself that can help you to recover from addiction.
6. Find a Power greater than yourself that is capable of removing the obsession and compulsion to use alcohol and other drugs.

7

I'LL LET THEM HELP ME

Will is the ability to make a decision and put it into action. In Step Three, recovering people decide to allow somebody else to make their decisions for them. To whom should you give that decision-making power? Someone who is more knowledgeable about making decisions. Somebody who knows how to recover. Why? Because you don't know what to do and are not in a frame of mind to figure it out. Everything you have tried has failed. You don't know what else to do. You need new help and you have to become willing to accept it.

Suppose you go to an attorney with a legal problem. The attorney recommends that you take steps A, B, and C, and you refuse repeatedly to follow his advice. What will the attorney do? He's going to ask you to leave, saying, "When you want help, come back."

I think of a Higher Power as an expert outside of myself with more experience and know-how than I have. The Higher Power is not just an expert. He or she is an expert who cares about me and would never do anything to harm me.

In Step Two, you find someone to give you an expert opinion on what you need to do, and in Step Three you agree to follow that advice. In Step One, you say, "I can't." In Step Two, "Somebody else can." In Step Three, you say, "I think I'll let them. I think I'll follow instructions." You don't have to like it; you just have to do it.

Some of the advice is very straightforward. You have to stop drinking and go to meetings. You have to get a sponsor and work the Steps. A.A. says it very well: "If you want what we've got, do what we did!" In other words, if you don't want sobriety, what A.A. has to offer, don't follow A.A.'s advice.

Someone may say, "But I think this is stupid!" It's not at all unusual for an A.A. member to look this newcomer right in the eye and say, "Yes, it is stupid, and I'm sober. How about you? Maybe if you would do the same stupid things that I did, you might also be sober."

Now you've stopped drinking, and you've been searching for a source of help. At Step Three, you follow directions; you start doing what you are told. Here's what that entails.

1. You decide to accept help from an outside source (the newly found Higher Power).

Your understanding of a Higher Power determines how you put this recommendation into action. I encourage people to recognize the A.A. program as one of their Higher Powers that, along with counseling and therapy, can provide clear direction.

I believe firmly that a spiritual Higher Power gives you courage, strength, and hope. Other people who have more experience in recovery give you the know-how. It is up to you to put that know-how into action. Turn it over to your Higher Power, but be willing to do the legwork.

2. You decide to use Twelve Step principles to guide your recovery from addiction.

The Twelve Steps provide clear, practical guidelines for what to do to recover, and it's in Step Three that alcoholics say, "I'm not going to drink. I'm going to go to meetings and get a sponsor. I'm going to read the Big Book and the Twelve and Twelve. I'm going to work the Steps and try to be rigorously honest. And I'm going to find out what else I need to do."

3. You seek appropriate professional help to deal with other problems that threaten sobriety.

In this Step recovering people seek out and follow expert advice in learning how to cope with problems that threaten their sobriety. If you're in severe withdrawal and need detox, you get it. If you're physically ill and need to go to the hospital, you check in. If you're manic-depressive and it's causing you to get drunk, you go for psychiatric treatment. If you've got a phobia and it prevents you from relating in A.A., you get it treated. If you were physically or sexually abused as a child, you get the treatment you need. You do whatever you need to do in order to stay sober and bond with a recovery program. But remember, if drinking and drugging was the primary problem, you must work your A.A. program first and then add these other treatments if you need them.

4. You use the spiritual principles of the Twelve Steps to govern the actions of your life.

In my mind, there is little difference between the words *spiritual* and *psychological*. The Greeks defined human beings as having two parts: the physical and the nonphysical. The nonphysical was described as spiritual.

Working a spiritual program means that you need to start paying attention to the nonphysical aspects of your being. You are practicing a spiritual program when you are trying to think clearly, logically, and rationally; or when you are looking inside to identify and communicate your feelings; or when you are trying to behave responsibly and "walk like you talk." You're also working a spiritual program when you attempt to improve your relationships with other people and bring greater harmony and cooperation into your life. In addition, the spiritual life also involves seeking an intuitive sense of a Power greater than yourself, a sense of the Ultimate Truth and Power that many people call God.

Most recovering people need to build a foundation for their spiritual lives. It starts with changing your thinking and behavior. Doing this causes your feelings to change, and your new feelings activate your intuition. This process allows you to experience the God of your understanding.

5. You participate consistently in a structured, long-term program of recovery.

If you have a problem with alcohol and drug use, you have to stop. In order to stop, you have to follow instructions. To follow instructions, you have to be around people who can give you instructions. And this means you need to consistently attend Twelve Step meetings, counseling, therapy, and whatever else is needed to ensure your recovery. The key word here is "consistently." You must make these things a part of your everyday lifestyle.

As a general rule of thumb, in the first year of recovery, you have to spend as much time in a recovery-oriented environment as you used to spend in a drinking-oriented environment. Every hour you once spent in a bar, you should match with time spent at meetings. That's rough, but you're not going to change your thinking unless you get enough contact hours of recovery under your belt.

6. You come to understand the ideas, principles, and recommendations of the Twelve Step program.

In order to make a decision to turn your will and your life over to the care of a Higher Power, you have to understand what your Higher Power wants you to do. If that Higher Power is going to be A.A., you start to explore, think about, understand, and personalize the principles of the Twelve Step program.

Everyone interprets the principles in slightly different ways. The important aspect is to try to understand what they mean and to work at developing a new, sobriety-centered philosophy about life and living. The Twelve Step principles are vague and general enough so they can serve as a projective device. You can read into them what you need at any moment in your recovery. And what you need to get from the Steps will change as you grow in sobriety. A big part of recovery is looking at the Steps, figuring out what they mean to you today, and then sharing that with others. If you are working the program correctly, your interpretation of the principles will change as you move ahead in your recovery.

7. You discipline yourself to review the Twelve Step principles when making important day-to-day decisions.

Twelve Step principles refer to the overall philosophy of life that is promoted by the Twelve Steps. Some of these principles include rigorous honesty, the willingness to admit and deal directly with problems as they occur, the willingness to seek outside help in solving problems, the ability to know

73

honestly your strengths and your weaknesses, the ability to use your strengths in the service of self and others, the willingness to ask others for help in areas of personal weakness.

Why is this necessary? Because you are in the habit of responding out of an addictive mind-set. Your addictive self is in charge, and to interrupt that mind-set, every time you are confronted with a decision, you have to ask yourself, "What principle applies here?" The easiest way for people to start doing this is by using the A.A. slogans.

Addictive principles are very different from Twelve Step principles. Addictive principles tell you that if it feels good, do it; lies don't count unless you get caught; honesty is not the best policy; and the only way to get ahead in life is to con and hustle.

In A.A. people learn a series of slogans that help them keep the basic Twelve Step principles in mind. When they're really upset, they use the slogan "Easy Does It." When they feel they can't live like this forever, they tell themselves that they don't have to do it forever—just "One Day at a Time." When they think they can't handle something, they can answer by saying, "I don't have to handle it—I Can Turn It Over."

When they feel as if they don't know what to do, they remember, "If you want what we got, do what we did." When they find someone who has the kind of life they want to have, they find out what that person did to get it, and they do what he or she tells them. If they do what that person did, they'll get what that person got.

Psychologically, this process is called "modeling." Neurolinguistic progamming (NLP) is based upon modeling—studying what people do to produce certain outcomes. A.A. is based on modeling, except that they don't use sophisticated terms in A.A. They say, "Stick with the Winners."

74

It's important that you look honestly and accurately at the person(s) you choose to emulate, because you may not in fact want what they've got, and if you do what they did, you'll get it whether or not you want it.

8. You learn to recognize when your own ideas are in conflict with Twelve Step principles.

You don't have to agree totally with the Twelve Steps. However, you do need to recognize where your own beliefs and perceptions are in conflict with the Steps, and then you have to choose. Do I follow the Twelve Step principles or my own ideas? There is no right or wrong here; there is simply a choice. After you choose, you take action; the action produces consequences, and you have an opportunity to learn. The logical consequences of your behavior are the greatest of all teachers. You begin to learn: "When I follow the Twelve Steps, things generally work, but when I follow my own ideas, my life often doesn't work."

One of the beautiful aspects of human beings is that we have rational minds: We can think. We have the ability to choose and we have volitional consciousness. We can choose what we do and we have a law of consequence. When we do things, something happens. And when something happens, we can think about it and learn from it. These results are activated by the A.A. program.

Recovering people think about what the program suggests they do and what they personally think they should do. They compare the two approaches, make a conscious choice, and put that choice into action. Then, life will give them a consequence. The choice they made will either work for them or it will work against them; if they are thinking people, that consequence will teach them something. You can learn from the consequences of your behaviors. And if you don't get drunk over it and block realization of the consequences, you will learn and grow.

Next comes the hardest part of the Third Step.

9. You follow Twelve Step principles even when it is difficult or when to do so forces you to change your normal ways of thinking and acting.

This is tough. Chemically dependent people don't like to be told what to do. But that is my understanding of what the Twelve and Twelve tells people to do. What I suggest people do, if they are willing, is to select some issue in their personal lives over which they are powerless and assess their willingness or resistance to using the first three Steps to deal with it.

We all have at least one thing we believe we are powerless over. For example, we'd like to be able to avoid some favorite foods so we could be a little thinner, or we want to stop smoking cigarettes. Perhaps we're in a relationship that's not working well, that we can't seem to improve or end. We can try applying the principles of the first three Steps to that issue.

The founders of A.A. made two brilliant moves: They wrote down the Twelve Steps and they numbered them. They suggested that people work the Steps in order. You don't need to teach a newcomer what all the Steps mean, but there is a saying in A.A.—"First Things First." You start with Step One.

You look at the issue in your life over which you are powerless, define the problem, and look at how you have tried to manage it thus far. You acknowledge that you don't have the knowledge, information, or frame of reference to understand or solve it; nor, in isolation, do you have the courage or the strength or the energy to handle it.

Then comes Step Two. You accept that there is somebody who has a bigger frame of reference, more knowledge, and more expertise than you do. You accept that there is a source of power, support, energy, courage, strength, and hope somewhere outside of you that can empower you to handle your problem. You start looking for that Higher Power and keep looking until you find it.

And then comes Step Three. You turn to that greater power for help and agree to follow directions. You look to a spiritual Higher Power for courage, strength, and hope. You look to experts on recovery, other recovering people with long-term sobriety, and trained professionals for the technical know-how.

Step One deflates the addictive ego by affirming, "I can't do it by myself." Step Two convinces you that somebody else can, so it instills hope that there is a way to recover, giving you the courage and strength to move ahead. Step Three shows you how to cooperate and move ahead in recovery. Recovering people strive for cooperation and interdependence with others: "I think I'll let them help."

As a result of these Steps, you learn a new sobriety centered standard of conduct based on solid principles instead of distortions of your ego. You align your behavior to this new standard and see what happens. You learn from it. That's what the first three Steps are all about.

POINTS TO REMEMBER

In completing Step Three you:

1. Accept help from an outside source (your newly found Higher Power).
2. Use Twelve Step principles to guide your recovery from addiction.

3. Use professional help to deal with other problems that threaten sobriety.
4. Use the spiritual principles of the Twelve Steps to govern the actions of your life.
5. Consistently participate in a structured long-term program of recovery.
6. Develop an understanding of the ideas, principles, and recommendations of the Twelve Step program.
7. Review these Twelve Step principles when making important day-to-day decisions.
8. Recognize when your own ideas are in conflict with Twelve Step Principles.
9. Follow Twelve Step principles even when it is difficult or when to do so forces you to change your normal ways of thinking and acting.

8

TAKING INVENTORY

The First Step teaches alcoholics that they are chemically dependent and that addictive use is destroying their lives. The Second Step teaches them that they lack the expert knowledge and the strength to solve the problem of addiction by themselves. The Third Step shows them that there is a source of courage, strength, and hope and a body of technical know-how that can show them the way out. Now they are ready for Step Four, learning how to take an inventory of current strengths and weaknesses.

It is frightening to take an honest look at yourself, perhaps for the first time in your life. Doing an inventory takes courage because you discover things about yourself that you don't want to know. Taking a Fourth Step inventory is a lot like shining a bright light into a cave. When you turn on the light, you can see all sorts of scary things crawling around inside.

A good Fourth Step is "searching." It challenges you to look at all aspects of yourself. It shows you that you are a fallible human being with strengths and weaknesses and that in order to recover, you must decide what you are bringing with you on your road to recovery so that you can build on your strengths while striving to overcome your weaknesses.

Step Four is a "moral" inventory, meaning that it pertains to the concept of right and wrong, "good" and "bad." It instructs you to answer such questions as: "Is my current way of life good for me or bad for me?" "Is it helping me or hurting me?" "Is it helping people I love or hurting them?" "Are my actions making me stronger or weaker in the long run of my life?"

My interpretation of what the Fourth Step says can be summarized in the five basic points that follow.

1. You recognize the need to complete a personal inventory of both strengths and weaknesses (character defects).

The first thing you must do is to recognize the need to take an inventory. In early recovery, most people are in denial. First they deny that they are chemically dependent; next they deny that their chemical use has damaged their lives; then they deny that they need outside help in order to recover. The first three Steps took care of that denial. But now they must break an even more deeply engraved form of denial—the denial of who they really are and what they really need to be happy.

Addicts of all kinds walk around with the delusion that "I am fine and everyone else is screwed up." No matter what goes wrong, there is someone else to blame. Step Four tells them that they need to stop blaming others and start taking personal responsibility for their actions and their consequences. If they are having problems staying sober, it is because they are doing something that doesn't work. The problem is that they don't know what it is they are doing that's ruining their sobriety. It takes a careful Fourth Step to figure it out.

Twelve Step programs ask you to learn how to separate your addictive self (the alcohol- and drug-centered thoughts, feelings, and behaviors) from your sober self (your sobriety-centered thoughts, feelings, and behaviors). But each Twelve Step program uses slightly different language. In most Twelve Step literature, the addictive self is called the "ego." Whenever I hear or read the word *ego*, I substitute the words *addictive self*.

The goal of a Fourth Step is to deflate the ego—or, in other words, to deflate the addictive self. The addictive self is marked by grandiosity (addicted people feel that they are more than or better than everyone else) and self-centeredness (they believe that they are the center of the universe and there is little room left for anyone or anything else). This grandiosity and self-centeredness often show up when taking a Fourth Step. Below is an example of the inventory completed by a grandiose alcoholic who had been sober for only three weeks.

"My strength is: tolerance in the midst of all of these morons and lunatics I have to cooperate with. My weakness is: my inability to get these people to live their lives the right way, the way God intended them to live—my way!"

Many alcoholics have another problem. They fluctuate between grandiosity (believing that they are better than everyone else) and self-pity (believing that they are worse than everyone else). The Fourth Step is designed to humble people. It is designed to show them who they really are in both their strengths and weaknesses. Then they can build upon those strengths while working to overcome the weaknesses.

It is difficult for a newcomer to complete a meaningful Fourth Step early in recovery. Perhaps he or she can learn what an inventory is and how to do it. He or she may even do a "dry run" Fourth Step inventory, but most of the inventories I have seen that were done within the first thirty days of sobriety are not Fourth Steps at all. They are First Steps in disguise.

When taking the First Step, you make a list of the problems that were directly caused by your addiction. This list generally describes what happened to you because of your addiction. The First Step focuses upon the problems caused by intoxication and withdrawal. It forces you to look at the consequences of your addiction-centered lifestyle. A Fourth Step inventory goes beyond this. It addresses the questions: "What is it about me that sets me up to become addicted?" "What is it that I am carrying with me into recovery that will set me up to relapse?"

The Fourth Step is designed to search out character defects that cause pain in sobriety. Character defects are actually a combination of four elements: mistaken beliefs, automatic irrational thoughts, painful feelings, and self-defeating behaviors.

Mistaken beliefs are ideas about ourselves, other people, and the world that we believe to be true but that are in reality false. Many recovering people, for example, make the mistake of believing that they are losers. Since they are losers anyway, why try? No matter how hard they work at recovery, they will eventually relapse. Why? Because that's what losers do.

Mistaken beliefs create *automatic irrational thoughts*. When things happen to us, old thoughts suddenly jump into our minds to allow us to make sense of what is going on. If you have mistaken beliefs, however, the automatic thoughts reflect an erroneous way of thinking about things.

Let us say you mistakenly believe that you are no good

and then someone falls in love with you. What kind of thoughts go through your head? You could very well ask yourself, "What's wrong with this person? I'm really no good. The fact that he or she loves me means this person must have pretty poor judgment."

Suppose you have a problem. An automatic thought might leap into your head that says, "Why bother? I'm a loser anyway! No matter what I do, things will stay screwed up."

If something good happens, you might wonder, "What's wrong here? This isn't right. Good things aren't supposed to happen to me. It is only a matter of time until I screw it up!"

These irrational thoughts cause *painful feelings*. Anger, rage, shame, guilt, depression, and anxiety are all common symptoms of an unresolved character defect. The irrational thinking and painful emotions drive the individual into uncontrollable *self-defeating behaviors*. These behaviors create problems and he or she can then use the problems as proof that his or her original mistaken belief was right.

The pain is caused by both irrational thinking and self-defeating behavior. The problem is that most of these thoughts and behaviors are automatic and unconscious. You do them without thinking. All you know is that you hurt, but you don't know what thoughts and behaviors are creating your pain.

To take a Fourth Step, you need to have some sobriety behind you because you are asked to look at serious personal problems, and that hurts. Most recovering people developed the habit of medicating pain by using alcohol and other drugs. If you take the Fourth Step too soon, the pain of becoming aware of your character defects can create a strong compulsion to use alcohol or other drugs to medicate the pain. Because of this, it is a good idea to have a solid recovery program that will keep you sober before you dig up a lot of pain by doing a Fourth Step.

When the Twelve Steps were written, they were numbered. Step Four is Step Four for a reason! You are supposed to work Steps One, Two, and Three before you take on the Fourth Step. Before you begin digging up your character defects, you need to have clearly established in your own mind that you are alcoholic (chemically dependent) and need to abstain from alcohol and all other drugs. You also need to learn how to ask for and receive help from others more knowledgeable in recovery.

The Fourth Step tells you to examine your strengths and weaknesses as a person and then identify the weaknesses that make you so miserable that you are likely to drink and drug in the future. Your character defects become apparent to you as you attempt to live the sober life. It is a period of sober living that makes a Fourth Step necessary. When you were involved in addictive use, you could easily manage the pain caused by your character defects. Relief was just a swallow away—a drink, a pill, a burst of compulsive activity, and the pain temporarily disappeared.

Unless you do an inventory to identify and change these destructive patterns, they linger and tend to get worse. In abstinence, this pain increases and it doesn't go away. Unless you can discover the specific thoughts, feelings, and behaviors that are driving the pain, it will just keep getting worse. A.A. calls these destructive thoughts, feelings, and behaviors "character defects." Psychologists call them "personality problems." Beneath each character defect are mistaken beliefs about self, others, and the world. You know the truth, or at least "the truth as you see it." You truly believe that you are right when in reality you are wrong. You have made a mistake in judging yourself and others and you don't even know it.

Why are some addicts grandiose? Because at times they truly believe, at the core of their being, that they are better than everyone else. Why do they beat themselves up and put themselves down at other times? Because a different mistaken belief has been activated. They have shifted from grandiosity to self-pity, and now they genuinely believe that they have less worth than others around them.

Why do alcoholics in early recovery tend to isolate themselves from other people? For some it is because they truly believe that people won't like them. For others it is because they truly believe that other people have little or nothing to offer.

This is why you have to do an in-depth inventory! You need to uncover these mistaken beliefs. You need to discover the nature of your wrongs, the fundamental core of mistaken beliefs that drives you into irrational thinking and self-defeating behavior. In order to do this, the inventory has to be searching and fearless. You do a searching inventory using critical questions that will bring to the surface your mistaken notions about yourself, others, and your life. Then you have to find the courage to answer those questions with complete honesty. There is nothing easy about taking a Fourth Step. For most, it is the most difficult thing they ever do in their life. As a result, many avoid taking this Step—or, when they do take it, they do it superficially.

I have known many people who have been sober five to ten years who have creatively avoided taking the Fourth Step. When asked about it, they say, "Well, I've done it in my head." When we ask them, "Have you written it down?" they say no. And if you ask them, "Have you developed a list of questions?" they say, "No, but I've got a generally good idea of who I am." Translated from the language of denial, that means, "No, I haven't taken a Fourth Step, but I don't want to admit it!"

A good Fourth Step doesn't result in a general idea of who you are. Instead, you know specifically who you are, what you are doing, and why you are doing it. A good Fourth Step makes you think about things you don't want to think about. It forces you to confront frightening and embarrassing aspects of yourself. In a good Fourth Step, most people discover that they have character defects that drive them to do crazy things in sobriety. The Fourth Step helps you understand the nature of the "addictive insanity" that follows you into sobriety.

2. You recognize and overcome the denial and excuses that blocked you from completing this inventory.

This is the next task. Just because you admit that you are chemically dependent doesn't mean that you have totally overcome your problem with denial. Denial follows most recovering people into sobriety, the only difference being the focus of your denial. When using chemicals, you deny your chemical addiction. When sober, you deny the character defects or personality problems that will drive you back to drinking. This denial is unconscious. You don't say to yourself, "I think I will deny thinking honestly about myself today!" You simply continue to think the way you have always thought, and you continue to believe you are the same type of person you were when drinking. You refuse to examine or change your addictive beliefs, attitudes, values, and thoughts.

To understand how denial can be unconscious, take a moment to think about your breathing. For the most part, breathing is an unconscious process. You do it all of the time, but you rarely think about it. It has become a habit. The only time you think about it is when there is not enough air around.

In the same way, you constantly deny much of your

reality. The only time you notice your denial is when the things you are denying flare up and cause you pain. And when that happens, you want to make the pain go away. You want to feel better without having to think better, act better, or relate better to other people. I want to feel better right now. I want to find something else that will do the same thing my drugs used to do for me. What do drugs and alcohol do? They make me feel better without having to think better, act better, or relate better to other people.

You recognize that you are using denial, that you're making excuses to keep from looking at yourself honestly. One of the biggest forms of denial is the use of compulsive behaviors. To keep your feelings turned off, you overeat, overwork, consume a lot of caffeine, or smoke a lot of cigarettes.

For a number of years, I worked in a treatment program where most of the staff smoked. You could always tell when a staff member was feeling something: The smokers would light up a cigarette; the compulsive overeaters would run to the cafeteria or pull a Twinkie out of a desk drawer; the compulsive overworkers would pull out their charts and start writing. Until you do a Fourth Step inventory, you continue to channel the pain of your mistaken notions into compulsive behaviors.

Getting ready to take a Fourth Step is difficult. You know you need to do an inventory, yet in spite of that knowledge, you resist it. How do you get past this?

3. You select a knowledgeable and experienced person (an A.A. sponsor, spiritual adviser, or counselor) to assist in the inventory process.

I believe this is vital. Do you try to shave or put on makeup without a mirror? No, you need a feedback system. If you are going to change your physical appearance, you need some instrument that will give you a reflection—that will make you physically visible to yourself. If you are trying to change yourself psychologically and spiritually, you need a mirror that will make you psychologically and spiritually visible to yourself. I call this "psychological visibility." You only get that in the reflection provided by other people being absolutely honest with you. So you need a mentor, a sponsor, or a spiritual or psychological adviser to help you take the Fourth Step. This adviser doesn't do the inventory for you; she or he will help you learn how to do it for yourself.

Once you select the person to help you design your inventory, you move into the next phase.

4. You develop a list of questions about your strengths and weaknesses to be used in completing the inventory.

This list of questions becomes a guide to use when completing the inventory. To be thorough, you need a method or a system. There are a lot of guidebooks available. The Hazelden catalog, from the Hazelden Foundation of Minnesota, lists a number of guides for doing a Fourth Step. The Big Book of A.A. provides a guide for doing the Fourth Step.

There is no one correct set of questions that need to be answered in a Fourth Step. The exact questions you use in your inventory need to be designed by you in cooperation with your sponsor or spiritual adviser. Somebody else has to help you ask, "What areas do I need to examine?"

So you take a look at the inventory guides. You take what fits for you, recognizing that different people have different problem areas that need to be the focus of a Fourth Step inventory. Each individual needs to develop an inventory guide for himself that will lead him to discover his character defects.

5. You complete the inventory by writing a list of your strengths and weaknesses.

First you identify your strengths and write them down. What are your assets? What do you have going for you that can act as a foundation for your recovery? Then you identify your personal weaknesses and write those down. What are your liabilities? What are the character defects that are likely to make you miserable in sobriety? One person put it this way: "To find out my character defects, I must ask myself why I am acting like a drunk even though I'm now sober."

It is important to write out the Fourth Step. If you don't write it down, you haven't really done it. By writing a clear list of your strengths and weaknesses, you are forced to confront yourself in writing. You are forced to write out an appraisal of yourself in black and white, to read it, and to make corrections. The process of writing forces you to start seeing yourself as others see you. When you think about these things, you can easily avoid and evade. When you write it down, you have to confront what you have written.

When you do a good Fourth Step, you are writing down secrets that you have never told anyone else, secrets you don't want to become common knowledge. If you would feel comfortable sharing your written inventory with just about anyone, you probably haven't identified your major defects. But if, as you are writing, a sense of terror develops at the core of your being and you become nervous about somebody finding your inventory and reading it, you probably are doing a meaningful Fourth Step.

When working on a "moral" inventory, your goal is to identify "the exact nature of your wrongs," not to make a list of every indiscretion you have committed in your life. For example, many people have a lot of guilt about their sexual behavior that they bring into recovery. If, in your Fourth Step, you write, "I had an affair with Sue and then with Shirley," that's a confession, not a Fourth Step.

A more helpful way to write a Fourth Step would be to say, "There is something inside of me that is driving me to be promiscuous." You should write down the nature of the wrong, not the specific details.

"Well, I stole a watch on Thursday and a wallet on Friday and a cuff-link set on Saturday." Is that a Fourth Step? No. "There is something compelling me to be a thief. There is some character defect that's driving me to steal." You need to identify that character defect—the nature of your wrongs.

"I lied to my child on Saturday, to my wife on Sunday, and to my boss Monday. And I'll never tell lies about those things again." Is that the important part? No. You'll lie about something else next time. The real issue is, there is some character defect that is compelling you to tell lies. That's the nature of the wrong. And that's the character defect that should be the target of a quality Fourth Step.

Many psychologists hate the words "character defects" because they get paid to call them "personality problems," but they are talking about the same thing. A character defect is a personality problem that is composed of automatic irrational thoughts, unmanageable feelings, and self-defeating behaviors.

Character defects operate on five levels. Level one is *situational*. Into what situation does the nature of your problem force you? The second level is *behavioral*. What behavior is your character defect driving you to do? The third level is *thinking*. What irrational thoughts are being created by the character defect? The fourth level is *feeling*. What unmanageable feelings and emotions are being created? The fifth level is belief—the *core mistaken belief*. This

90

is the basic character defect that fuels the whole problem. "What is the fundamental mistaken belief at the core of your value system that's driving you to behave in this manner?" It is these core mistaken beliefs for which you search in a thorough Fourth Step inventory.

For example, why would you be compelled to be promiscuous? Let's examine the levels at which this character defect operates. On a situational level, you go cruising. You put yourself in situations where you are around people who turn you on. Something inside of you compels you to act differently and you change your behavior by beginning to flirt. Then your irrational thinking fires off: "Boy, it would be wonderful if he/she would go to bed with me! I'd be a better person and all of my problems would go away!" Then come the feelings. The potential risk and adventure cause your adrenaline to kick in and you become excited. The sexual fantasies cause your sex hormones to pump. What's underneath all of this? It could be several core mistaken beliefs. A common one is "Promiscuous behavior will make me a real man [or a real woman]!" This belief is mistaken, because being a man or woman has to do more with character than with sexual behavior. Others are driven by a different core belief: "Promiscuous behavior will solve my problems." In reality, most people find out that promiscuous sexuality creates more problems than it ever solves. Other people mistakenly believe that having sex with many different partners can somehow make them feel whole or complete. Or they mistakenly believe that if they can find the right love partner, everything in life suddenly will be satisfying.

For many, taking the Fourth Step for the first time is a powerful, life-changing experience—an experience of fear and courage, pain and relief, doubt and absolute faith. For the Fourth Step to work, you must be fearless and searching. If you do a Fourth Step halfheartedly, there will be little personal benefit. "No pain, no gain!" If you are willing to take a truly honest inventory, you will find not only pain but also a tremendous source of long-term relief.

POINTS TO REMEMBER

In completing Step Four you:

1. Come to believe that you need to do a personal inventory of your strengths and weaknesses.
2. Overcome the denial and excuses that blocked you from completing this inventory.
3. Select a knowledgeable and experienced person (an A.A. sponsor, spiritual adviser, or counselor) to assist in the inventory process.
4. Develop a list of questions about your strengths and weaknesses to be used in completing the inventory.
5. Complete the inventory by writing a list of your strengths and weaknesses.

9

SHARING

STEP FIVE
Admitted to God, to ourselves, and to another human being the exact nature of our wrongs.

I believe that the first four Steps must be worked thoroughly in order for a Fifth Step to provide deep insight and emotional relief. This is because each of the previous Steps is designed to resolve a problem that, if unresolved, prevents the Fifth Step from working. If you have done a superficial job on the First Step, you are still doubting your alcoholism and thinking you can control your drinking. If this is the case, then honestly discussing your character defects with others will create pain that can activate compulsion and craving.

If your Second Step was incomplete, you won't really believe there is a source of help that can remove your obsession with booze and drugs. As a result, you will not trust the Steps or any specific sponsor. Without trust and the willingness to be honest, the Fifth Step will be minimally effective.

If you only toyed with the Third Step, you still believe you have to go it alone and have trouble asking for and receiving help from others. If this is the case, how can you ever ask another member of the program to hear your Fourth Step?

In short, if the first three Steps were not completed thoroughly, your addict-alcoholic ego is still intact. If this is true, you will get hung up on the Fourth Step, because your addictive ego will get in the way. Your addictive grandiosity will exaggerate your strengths while your addictive ego will minimize or block out your weaknesses. While this is happening, you will be unable to be rigorously honest with yourself or anyone else. The result will be a superficial Fourth Step and then a superficial Fifth Step.

The Fifth Step builds upon the foundation created by thoroughly working the first four Steps. The First Step convinces alcoholics that they are addicted, cannot safely use alcohol or other drugs, and need to abstain. Step Two convinces them that there is a source of courage, strength, and hope, and a body of technical know-how that can help them to stay sober one day at a time. Step Three allows them to move beyond their addictive grandiosity and ask for and receive help from others. Step Four guides them in creating a written list of strengths and weaknesses that captures the essence of who they are as people. Their core strengths become their foundation in building a life of sobriety. Their weaknesses become a target for personal growth and change.

When you have succeeded in identifying your core mistaken beliefs and your character defects, then you discuss these things with other people. Your refusal to do so will keep you sick. In order to change, you must share what you have learned about yourself by doing a Fourth Step. It's self-defeating to keep it a secret. One recovering person put it this way: "We are only as sick as our secrets." Why? Because keeping secrets forces us to live in isolation. If you don't know yourself, you can't really know anybody else. Your addictive self keeps you out of touch with yourself and isolated from other people. The Fifth Step is the path out of isolation.

First, you confide the results of your inventory to your Higher Power—your source of courage, strength, and hope. Then you find at least one other human being in whom you can confide. You share the outcome of your inventory and listen to their feedback.

It is important to remember that you are not merely reciting a litany of sins. You are describing the core character defects in your personality that drive you to do things repeatedly even though you know they are not good for you. And you can't complete that inventory process alone. You have to involve at least one other person. How do you do this?

1. You acknowledge that you are living in isolation from other people and that this isolation prevents you from achieving a comfortable sobriety.

You're going to meetings and you're around people, yet you still feel isolated. Why? Are you being rigorously honest? If you can't be honest with yourself, you can't be honest with other people. To get close to others, you must share honest knowledge about who and what you are. And you can't do that when you don't know who you really are.

2. You acknowledge that your ego (your addictive self) is preventing you from sharing the results of your inventory (your deepest thoughts, feelings, beliefs, and problems) with other people.

Your Fourth Step inventory reflects your deepest thoughts, feelings, beliefs about yourself and other people. It clearly describes the problems that are creating pain and discomfort in your sobriety. It exposes the things that cause you to feel shame, guilt, and fear. Your addictive self wants to keep your defects a secret. Why? Those core character defects are necessary to justify your next relapse. If you don't deal with the defects, they will deal with you by creating so much pain and discomfort that you may start to say to yourself, "If this is sobriety, who needs it?"

So your addictive self will try to convince you that something awful will happen if you share your inventory with someone else. The addictive self will try to scare you into silence and deception, because only then can your addiction come back to life. This moves you to the next task.

3. You acknowledge that it is self-defeating to keep the results of your inventory secret by refusing to discuss it with another person.

You have discovered critical issues that have the power to destroy your serenity and drive you back into addictive use. What you have learned is critical. It reflects the core of your own personal reality, the essence of who you believe you are. Since the inventory is a mixture of good and bad, most people are terrified of letting anyone else know what they have found, because they are afraid that he or she will abandon them, hate them, or at least refuse to love or care about them. They fear that they will be shamed, humiliated, and destroyed. In order to recover, you have to challenge this fear. You have to have the courage to risk exposing yourself to another trusted human being to see what happens. You must recognize this fear of vulnerability for what it is—part of your addiction. You must acknowledge that it's self-defeating to hide important problems, keep painful memories a secret, and hide your feelings and beliefs from others.

4. You become willing to confide the results of your inventory to another person.

Notice, I didn't say, "I became excited and enthused about sharing these results." More correctly, I might say, "With a terror-stricken heart, I realized that I had to take a chance in sharing my inventory with somebody else." You have to confide the results of your inventory or the healing process of the Fourth and Fifth Steps doesn't work.

5. You select a person in whom you are willing to confide.

Taking a Fifth Step is a critical act of trust. It is important to identify a trustworthy person in whom you can confide, because if you don't trust this person, you can't be absolutely honest. In this way, the Fifth Step helps you grow by teaching you the nature of trust. To take a Fifth Step, you must become willing to allow another person to discover the essence of your being. In selecting someone to listen to a Fifth Step, you must answer two critical questions: "Are there trustworthy people in the world?" "Do I believe that I can be rigorously honest and not get hurt in the process?"

When you do the Fourth and Fifth Steps, you give that other person the power and opportunity to hurt you, and that's scary. Unfortunately, there are some people with whom you should *not* share your Fourth Step, because, given the opportunity to hurt you, they will. Don't choose a person with only three days of sobriety, a sober psychopath, or someone with grave emotional problems. Select someone you admire and respect. Most important, choose someone who is not a gossip and will honor the confidences you are about to share.

"What if I don't know anybody like that?" If you don't, you're not ready to do a Fifth Step. To get ready, you must find that trustworthy person. That means you have to go to a lot of meetings and listen to a lot of stories.

Once you have found a trustworthy person, you can move ahead.

6. You discuss the results of your inventory openly and honestly with the chosen person in private.

Here is one approach. Ask the person you have selected to talk with you privately after an A.A. meeting. Explain that you have selected this person to hear your Fourth Step and tell him or her why you made the choice. A typical request might be: "Tyrone, I'm getting to the point in my program where I need to take a Fifth Step. I have already written out a Fourth Step inventory. I've been listening to you in meetings and I heard you tell your story a couple of weeks ago. I really like the program you put together for yourself. Your experiences seem similar to mine and I think you'll be able to understand and help me sort out my inventory. Are you willing to do it?"

Although most Twelve Step members are willing to hear the Fifth Step of other members, some are not. If you are refused, don't take it personally. That person may have some personal difficulties that would interfere with his or her ability to listen to and support you. The person may be sponsoring so many other people that he or she just doesn't have the time. Start looking again and find another person.

Doing a Fifth Step takes time. It is generally best to schedule at least two hours in a private place without interruptions. The following example is a summary of what happens in a typical Fifth Step. Angie is listening to Pat's Fifth Step inventory.

"Let me ask you a question to get started," says Angie. "Do you have any fears about reading your Fifth Step to me?"

"I'm nervous," admits Pat with a smile on her face. "I've never done anything like this before and I feel silly."

"That's exactly the way I felt when I took my Fifth Step," Angie laughs. "Don't worry, it'll get easier once we get started. Tell me, what questions or inventory guide did you use to get ready?"

Pat tells her that she prepared by reviewing the seven cardinal sins of sloth, lust, anger, pride, envy, greed, and gluttony.

"Which one would you like to start with?" asks Angie.

"Let's start with pride," says Pat hesitantly. "It's the easiest to talk about. I've always wanted people to think well of me. I wanted them to respect me and think that I was okay. But somehow, deep inside, I never thought they did. I thought they could see right through me and see how bad off I really was. So I tried to be better than they. You know, tried to show off and things like that. Every chance I get, I try to show people that I'm better. I brag a lot. I try to get people to talk about what I know, and I avoid dealing with anything that will make me look stupid. It feels good when I do something right—in fact, I love it. But I tend to put other people down. I get threatened when they can do things better than I can, so I avoid them."

"What does it feel like when you are being prideful?" Angie asks.

"It really feels pretty good! I feel important. It's like I'm the queen of the ball or on center stage. I feel better than everyone else, so I don't have to be afraid of anybody."

"So people scare you?" Angie asks. "They used to scare me, too. And it sounds like you're happiest when you're in a one-up position. But I'm wondering—doesn't that get lonely?"

"It gets real lonely," stammers Pat. "I also feel funny because it seems so easy to con people—so easy to convince them I'm queen of the ball when I really feel scared and awkward. It's been that way all of my life. I've always felt like I have to prove myself. I hate it. Why can't I just belong and be like everyone else?"

"It sounds like your pride is driven by something. What is that something?"

"I guess my pride is driven by the need to prove I'm okay," admits Pat.

"So you believe you're not okay? Deep inside, do you believe there is something wrong with you?"

"Yes, I do, and it's not easy to admit." Pat is sullen. She feels like crying but won't let herself.

"How does this hook up with your drinking and drugging?" asks Angie.

"When I was drinking, it was easier to put down my feelings. I used cocaine—a lot. The coke made me feel like Superwoman. When I was on coke, I didn't just feel better than everyone else. I knew that I was better."

"And now that you're sober, is it hard to get that same feeling?" questions Angie.

"Yes, it is! And sometimes I want to feel that way so bad I'm willing to do almost anything."

As this dialogue shows, a Fifth Step can get intense. Notice that Angie isn't telling Pat anything. She is asking questions. She is trying to give Pat permission to push deeper into her feelings and to tell more. Notice also that she is not judgmental. And she shares her own experience by saying such things as, "I know what you mean because it was like that for me, too."

This example is just one of many ways in which sponsors guide people through a Fifth Step. Each sponsor has his or her own unique style. There is no right or wrong way to hear a Fifth Step, as long as the conversation is based upon a deep sense of respect and love. It is this love that one recovering addict feels for another that drives the healing process of A.A.

After reviewing the entire inventory, you move to the next level.

7. You listen to and accept advice and direction from the person in whom you confided your inventory.

In essence, you are saying, "Here I am. This is me! I'm naked in front of you. You see all there is to see. My strengths and my weaknesses. Here it is." You then take a deep breath and say, "Now tell me, what do you think and how do you feel?" Sometimes people sit there in terror waiting for the answer, because they believe that they are going to be judged. More typically, however, the listener looks you in the eye and says something like this: "You know, you're not much different from me, and I feel really close to you. I appreciate your willingness to take a risk. By sharing your inventory with me, you have helped me to grow. By listening to you, I've been able to see myself and my own defects more clearly. Thank you for being part of my recovery."

Sharing a Fifth Step generates caring, warmth, and love. A bond of trust often develops. And with this trust comes the ability to hear feedback. The sponsor often will say something like this: "As we were talking about your inventory, some of the things you said rang true for me, and I said 'right on.' Here's what they were.... But you also said some things that didn't ring true. It may be just me, but as you said them, I felt uncomfortable. It was as if you weren't really being honest with yourself, as if you were just skimming the

101

surface. As my grandfather would say, 'This smells rotten.' I don't know if it is or not. I might be wrong, but I just want to share that with you if you are willing to listen."

When the feedback is over, the sponsor often ends by saying something like this: "I think you're great for sharing this with me and for listening to my feedback. Sharing with you has helped me, too. I've got a lot to think about because of your honesty. Some of my own character defects have been hooked, and that's good, because now I get a chance to work on them."

A Fifth Step becomes a ritual of deep personal sharing: You read your Fifth Step to someone because you need to learn about yourself and grow; that person listens to your Fifth Step because it helps him or her to grow; both of you benefit from helping each other to stay sober. A.A. is a selfish program based upon love.

POINTS TO REMEMBER

In completing Step Five you:

1. Acknowledge that you are living in isolation from other people and that this isolation prevents you from achieving a comfortable sobriety.
2. Acknowledge that ego (the addictive self) is preventing you from sharing the results of your inventory (your deepest thoughts, feelings, beliefs, and problems) with other people.
3. Acknowledge that it is self-defeating to keep the results of your inventory and other distressing and humiliating memories secret by refusing to discuss them with another person.

4. Become willing to confide the results of your inventory to another person.
5. Select a person in whom you are willing to confide.
6. Discuss the results of your inventory openly and honestly with this person in private.
7. Listen to and accept advice and direction from the person in whom you confided the results of your inventory.

10

THE WILLINGNESS
TO CHANGE

> ### STEP SIX
>
> Were entirely ready to have God remove all these defects of character.

Step Six is tricky, and it can be difficult to understand. The first part of the Step says that we "were entirely ready." You can't change until you are ready to do so, and this Step recognizes that fact. The next part of the Step says that you "have God remove all these defects of character."

This baffled me. I always thought that recovering people had to change, that they had to do the legwork. Initially, I thought that this was a passive step, telling the alcoholic just to sit back, do nothing, and wait for God to intervene. But I later changed this view.

I now believe that God removes the alcoholic's defects as the result of a process. First you have to identify the defect that you want removed. This occurs in Step Four. Then you acknowledge that character defect to your Higher Power in order to find courage, strength, and hope, and to other people with experience in recovery in order to find expert advice on getting rid of that defect. This occurs in Step Five.

Then you must develop a deep belief that you can solve the problem and become willing to do so. This is the Sixth Step.

The God of my understanding doesn't do the "legwork" for others. Many chemically dependent people want others to do the work of recovery for them, and they take this addictive way of thinking and apply it to their Higher Power. In the process, they create the image of a codependent God who will allow them to be irresponsible while miraculously taking away the resulting problems. The God of my understanding is not codependent. My God allows recovering people to experience the consequences of their own behavior, to learn from their mistakes, and to make choices in order to do what is necessary to correct the problems.

There is no such thing as a "free lunch" in life. God doesn't pay the tab for you. Instead, God gives you the courage to pay the price you need to pay in order to get out. You can do just about anything you want to do in life if you are willing to pay the price—and that's the big *if*. What makes you willing to pay the price? I believe it's the God of your understanding. And if you are hooked into a Higher Power that doesn't give you the courage necessary to get free from a character defect, perhaps you need to consider trading in your Higher Power for one that works a little better.

At the heart of Step Six is the personal struggle to understand who God is and how God operates in your life. You can select your own concept of a Higher Power. That's what the A.A. program is about. For most recovering people who work the program, the concept of God changes over time. The concept of God that saved them three days sober is very different from their concept of God that saves them three years sober. God doesn't change, but their understanding of Him does. People get into trouble when they fail to separate the difference between the Higher Power and "my understanding" of the Higher Power. Many of them enshrine a mistaken notion of God and then insist that the world should believe as they do.

To me, it is helpful to think about the word *God* as an acronym for "Good Orderly Direction." God created an orderly universe and gave human beings a rational mind to figure how the universe works. He also gave us the ability to make choices and a law of consequence that allows us to learn from our choices. As a result, we think, choose, act, and experience the consequences.

Those consequences can be regarded as a message from God that teaches us vital lessons. If the consequences of our actions produce growth, love, and serenity, God is saying, "Well done!" If the consequences lead to progressive pain and dysfunction, God is saying, "There is something wrong here! You had better examine your approach to life and change what you are doing!"

When I discussed this Step with Father Martin, he said, "God gives us the courage, the strength, and the means whereby to correct our character defects. But we've got to do the correcting." In A.A., this concept is called "turning it over, but doing the legwork." You turn your self-defeating behavior over to God to gain the insight or the inspiration to know what you need to do, and the courage and strength to carry it out. Then you have to do the hard part—the work.

Father Martin teaches that God always answers prayer. If you pray, "God, please make me a doctor," God answers by saying, "Go to medical school!" If you pray to God to fix your marriage, God answers by saying, "Go to marriage counseling!" If you pray, "Please fix my compulsive over-eating," God says, "Get into an eating-disorder program."

So it's really very simple. You ask for guidance so you

can discover what needs to be done, and then you ask for the inspiration, courage, and strength to do it. But since you have free will, you can do what you want. Once you have come this far, you are free to do the necessary legwork or not. You have a choice. The choices you make will have consequences, and you are free to learn from those consequences.

A recovering alcoholic named Bert couldn't keep his house clean. As a result, he lived in a messy house, and it was driving him crazy. He decided to handle the problem by turning it over to his Higher Power, so he prayed to God to clean his house.

When this didn't work, Bert talked to his sponsor and realized he was misinterpreting the role of his Higher Power in recovery. Bert revised his thinking by coming to the conclusion that God was not going to clean his house. He then adopted the belief that since his house was a mess, it must be God's will that he should live in a messy house. So he began to pray to God to make him feel comfortable living in the mess.

That didn't work either, and finally Bert began to realize that if he wanted to stop living in a mess, he would need to pray to God for the courage and strength to clean up his own house.

Psychologically, the Sixth Step is very interesting. Recovering people live consciously aware of their character defects and their consequences. This conscious awareness makes them sick and tired of their defects. Then they get ready to do what is necessary to get rid of them. There is no "magic" in Step Six. You just get "sick and tired of being sick and tired." You get sick and tired of living with the character defects that are messing up your life and you become willing to change.

Once you become consciously aware of your defects and

live with that conscious awareness for a while, you become motivated to learn what you can do to get rid of those defects. Then you go about gathering the courage and strength to do what you need to do. This leads you into Step Seven.

Many people struggle with Steps Six and Seven, and there are many ways of interpreting them. Each different interpretation rests upon the concept of spirituality that you choose to embrace. I believe in a rational spirituality, one that teaches that spiritual truth and rational truth are the same and result from using different faculties of the creative mind. I believe that God created an orderly universe and gave human beings a rational mind that can be used to understand it. The God of my understanding would never order you to turn off your mind as a condition of salvation.

God also gave individuals the power to choose and the ability to experience and think about the consequences of their choices. God seems to operate in life by expecting people to learn from the consequences of their behavior and to make changes. God gives them the courage and strength to change, but they must do the changing. The God of my understanding would never alter the natural order of the universe because a recovering alcoholic made a mess of his or her life and was unwilling to do the work necessary to clean up the mess.

I know many people who believe that God directly intervenes to make recovery happen. These interventions are often referred to as "miracles." I know many sober alcoholics who believe that they recovered through the direct and miraculous intervention of God. I have seen alcoholics who were hopeless by all standards of medicine and psychotherapy, yet they managed to recover through the A.A. program and a belief in God. As a result, I don't believe there are any hopeless alcoholics. Recovery will happen when you start to believe in the possibility of recovery and become willing to tap into a source of courage, strength, and hope by praying for and expecting a miracle. But, as A.A. wisdom teaches, recovery requires more than just prayer. Pray for potatoes, but be willing to pick up a hoe and start planting.

Working Step Six involves the completion of six tasks.

1. You acknowledge that in sobriety your character defects often drive you into self-defeating behaviors with problematic consequences.

Even in sobriety, many people feel compelled to act out in self-defeating and destructive ways. This compulsion is created by their character defects. In order to remove the compulsion, they must remove the character defects that drive them. And before they can remove the character defects, they must become willing to do so. This is the work of the Sixth Step—to make people willing to give up the character defects that make them miserable in sobriety.

Character defects drive recovering people right back into thinking, acting, and relating to others like a drunk or a drug addict, even though they are no longer drinking or drugging. In other words, character defects create dry drunks. These behaviors come naturally, and they are difficult to change. It's easy for sober people to think, feel, act, and relate to others just as they did when they were drinking and drugging. It's much more difficult to act in accordance with sobriety-centered values.

In A.A., conscious contact with sobriety-centered living is called "serenity." And serenity does not mean a drug-induced stupor in sobriety, as many people tend to think. "Serenity? Is that like you feel when you are on opium?" No. Serenity means complete acceptance of your full range of emotionality. It's being able to feel what you feel when you feel it, being able to fully acknowledge it and to know that it's okay.

I can be really angry and still be serene. Why? Because I know the anger is okay and I know I can deal with it without hurting myself or others. Or I can be sad and be serene. Why? Because serenity is the primal background acceptance that what I feel is valid. It's real and I don't need to be ashamed of it or feel guilty about it.

Serenity is also the knowledge that what I feel and what I do about my feelings are two different things. Take, for example, Lou, who was separated from his wife but wanted to be reconciled. One evening he met an attractive woman who flirted with him and invited him out to dinner. Lou accepted.

Over dinner, it became obvious that there was a strong sexual chemistry between them, and the young lady asked Lou if he would like to go up to her apartment. Lou said no and the young lady was shocked.

"I'm sorry!" she said. "I must have misinterpreted what's been going on. I thought there were strong feelings between us."

"You're right," said Lou. "There are strong feelings between us, and it would really feel great to go up to your place and make love with you tonight. A part of me really wants to do that. But I am a married man, and even though we're separated, I want to get my wife back. That's my number-one priority right now."

Lou paused for a moment and then said, "What I feel and what I do about my feelings are two different things. I know what I feel, and it's wonderful! But I'm not going to act on it because it's not in my best interest. I am not going to sacrifice what I want most for what I want at the moment."

That's serenity—the ability to know the difference between what you need to do for your recovery and what you want to do that will cause problems. When Lou got home, he had a feeling of regret that he had lost an experience. But he accepted that as normal. There are always going to be losses. That's part of life.

What would Lou have done if he had not been in a sobriety-centered state of mind? With sober people, it's ready, aim, fire. For people in an addictive mind-set, it's ready, fire, aim, blow off your foot, and blame somebody else.

If Lou had been following addictive thinking, he would have jumped into bed with the woman, his wife would have divorced him, and he would have said, "It's all her fault! If I had a reasonable wife, she wouldn't have left me in the first place. Then I wouldn't have been vulnerable, so it's all her fault!"

2. You acknowledge that your character defects give you temporary pleasure that you enjoy.

Character defects aren't all bad—they have an "up" side and a "down" side. They feel good and they hurt, though not at the same time. They make you feel good now and you pay the price later. As a result, they weaken you over the long run of your life.

When the pain comes, you tend to use the same behavior again to obtain temporary relief. When more pain results, you do it again, but now you have to do it harder, faster, and more often. Consequently, you become addicted. Character defects are addictive.

"Self will run riot" is the phrase used in A.A. I heard a person say, "I get addicted to anything I do that feels good and that I have to do more than once." Chemically dependent people have a tendency to go to excess, to go to extremes. You need to acknowledge that there is an "up" side to your defects. At times you really enjoy them.

112

3. You identify the character defects that you are ready to give up.

One way to do a Sixth Step is to make a list of your character defects, including the problems and benefits experienced from each of them.

It should come as no surprise that character defects cause you problems. But many people deny the problems. They prefer to look the other way or to blame the problems on someone or something else. To get ready to give up a character defect, you must carefully examine the problems it causes.

Once you can see the problems of a character defect, you need to look at the benefits or secondary gains that you receive from keeping that defect alive. Many people are surprised when I ask them to look at the benefits of having a character defect. "Aren't character defects all bad?" they ask. The answer is no. You gain something from keeping these defects alive or you would give them up. Before you can get free from a character defect, you must figure out the benefits that you are getting from it and learn how to get those benefits in some other way.

You then compare the problems and the benefits associated with each defect so you can decide whether you are willing to do what is necessary to give it up. Remember, giving up a defect involves both stopping acting it out and doing something else that will produce the same benefits in a healthy way without producing the pain and problems. Once you have identified your character defects and the problems and benefits associated with each, you are ready to decide which of the defects you are ready to give up and which you choose to keep.

So you divide your character defects into two lists. List 1 contains the defects you are willing to give up and list 2

113

contains the defects that you choose, for the time being, to keep.

Frank, for example, was grandiose. He truly believed he was smarter and more important than anyone else. As a result, he put other people down and pushed them away. This made him lonely. So why did Frank continue being grandiose? "I enjoy it," he told his therapy group. "When I am into my grandiosity, I feel powerful and alive. I feel like I am important and really count for something. If I were to give up my grandiosity, I would feel insignificant and unimportant."

In order to become willing to give up his grandiosity, Frank needed to find other ways to feel powerful, alive, and important. So he tried to help others by listening and supporting them, rather than by lecturing and demanding that they do it his way. Frank found that he felt important and that others began to enjoy being around him. He began to feel that he really belonged. This made him feel alive and significant. As he learned how to help others without imposing his will on them, he was able to give up his grandiosity.

4. You ask for the willingness to do what is necessary to remove the character defects that you are ready to give up.

I don't believe Step Six is a magical process of asking and then having God whisk away your defects. The God of my understanding doesn't operate that way. God gave me a rational brain and volitional consciousness, and He says, "Choose and act, and you'll learn whether you did the right thing by the consequences."

The Sixth Step is a process of living consciously and learning from the consequences of your behavior. Character defects cause painful consequences. If you are consciously aware of your character defects and the consequences they

114

consistently cause you, you eventually become sick and tired of the fact that you are killing yourself. And once you are aware of the destructiveness of these defects, you become willing to do something about them.

5. You identify the character defects that you are still unwilling to give up.

Many people have character defects that they really like. The secondary gains are so important to them that they are not ready to give them up. Sure, they cause them problems. But they also make them feel good.

Recovering people become consciously aware of how they choose to live. They turn *on* their consciousness—they don't turn it off. Sobriety is the process of turning on lights, not turning them off. Addictive thinking turns off consciousness; sobriety-centered thinking turns it on.

They become aware. They can see more clearly, feel more intensely, and experience more fully. Reality becomes amplified, magnified, and intensified. In the Sixth Step, the Higher Power energizes you to become fully aware and conscious of the reality of existence and then gives you the courage to face it.

Step Six says "were entirely ready," and it is while you are living in full consciousness that you are choosing to do things that make you feel good or that hurt you. It is knowing the mechanism of that choice and living consciously with what you do that makes you ready to change. In A.A. terms, "We get sick and tired of being sick and tired."

And that realization applies not only to drinking. It applies to every individual character defect. Until you are sick and tired of what that character defect is doing to you, you are not ready to change.

6. You ask for the willingness, at some time in the future, to give up the character defects you still choose to hold onto.

You may not be willing to give up some of your defects today, but you are hopeful that you will become willing to give them up at some time in the future. In essence, you say, "I am not willing to do this today, but please make me willing to do it at some time in the future."

Stan, for example, was a recovering alcoholic who directed a large treatment center that had more than a hundred employees. Stan's character defect was grandiosity. He had a need for power and he used it. He would manipulate employees and expected blind obedience from them. He needed other people to make him feel important. Even after seven years of sobriety, he could not envision himself living without that power. He couldn't say, "At some point in the future, I'm going to be willing to give this up." Life without that "power intoxication" was incomprehensible to him.

It took Stan four years of working a Sixth Step—living in conscious awareness of the price he was paying for that power—to develop the courage and strength to change. During those four years, the stress was literally killing him, but he hung on. Why? His grandiosity would not let him leave. His pride wouldn't let him say, "I can't handle this; I need something else." He ended up getting sick and going to an intensive-care unit as a result of a stress-related physical breakdown. He spent ten days thinking about the price he was paying for the power he was wielding. Finally he decided it wasn't worth it. He became entirely ready to leave and to find a new job.

Once you become ready, it is time to move onto the Seventh Step, where you actually give up these defects of character.

116

POINTS TO REMEMBER

In completing Step Six you:

1. Acknowledge that in sobriety your character defects often drive you into self-defeating behaviors with problematic consequences.
2. Acknowledge that your character defects give you temporary pleasure that you enjoy.
3. Identify the character defects that you are ready to give up.
4. Ask for the willingness to do what is necessary to remove the character defects that you are ready to give up.
5. Identify the character defects that you are still unwilling to give up.
6. Ask for the willingness, at some time in the future, to give up the character defects that you still choose to hold onto.

11

ASKING

God removes shortcomings by mobilizing people to do what they need to do to fix their problems. I believe that the Serenity Prayer, which often is used at Twelve Step meetings, captures the essence of what Step Seven is all about: "God, grant me the serenity to accept the things I cannot change, the courage to change the things I can, and the wisdom to know the difference." Let's use this prayer as a guide for understanding how Step Seven works.

It starts with the words "God [or your Higher Power], grant me the serenity to accept the things I cannot change." God, as we have discussed, is the source of courage, strength, and hope on which people center their recovery. They have to look outside of their addictive frame of reference by turning to their Higher Power for help in solving their problems. What their Higher Power gives them is serenity, the state of mind that allows them to accept themselves fully as they are in all of their strengths and weaknesses. When people are serene, they believe on a deep level that it is okay to be themselves and that their lives are unfolding as they should unfold.

They are also told to "accept the things [we] cannot change." Acceptance is the belief that things are okay without our interference or meddling. Once alcoholics know that they are powerless, they need to turn themselves over to God and stop trying to exercise control. You are not the keeper of the universe. There are things that you cannot handle and it is okay for you to stop trying. Why can't you control everything? Because you are a fallible human being with limitations. That is the way you were born and that is the way you will die. You can't be all things to all people, and you don't have to try to be.

Some people read the first part of the Serenity Prayer and stop there. They come to believe that "all I have to do is turn my problems over to God and He will fix them." This interpretation of "turn it over" translates into "I don't have to do anything!" Is this really what the Serenity Prayer is telling us? I don't think so. If turning it over meant that "I am not responsible to do anything," the Serenity Prayer would have to be rewritten to read, "God, grant me the serenity to accept everything because there is nothing that I have the power to change."

We do have the power to change some things in our lives. The next part of the Serenity Prayer asks for "the courage to change the things [we] can." People need courage to do those things that are within their power to do. They need to identify their responsibilities and meet them whenever possible. They must do certain things in recovery—not because they feel good, but because they are their responsibility.

The last part is the most difficult: "the wisdom to know the difference." How do you know when you are wasting energy on things that you can't change, versus when you are operating within your sphere of authority and influence? As human beings we are limited; we can't always make a distinction. How can we know when to invest energy and when to "turn it over"? This is a primary struggle of all recovering people—acquiring the wisdom to know the difference.

So what exactly do you do when working the Seventh Step?

1. You regularly examine your goals in life and what you are doing to achieve them.

Recovering people must know what they want out of sobriety, and this means knowing what they value. What is truly important? You have a limited amount of time, energy, and resources. What should you invest in and what should you let go?

Step Six has taught you that you are often driven by your character defects to do things that are in fact of little value to you. I recommend that people write out a list of values and goals, defining what they value in sobriety and what they want to do in order to make those values come alive. The first temptation is to set goals to change things outside of yourself: I want a better job, I want to make more money, I want to be more important and powerful. There is nothing wrong with setting external goals, but that is not the point of Step Seven, which asks you to set goals in the one area that is of primary importance.

2. You recognize that character building (psychological growth) and the development of spiritual values are the only meaningful and enduring goals in life.

Psychological and spiritual growth is what really counts. It is imperative that recovering people build character if they are to become high-value people who are worthy of love, respect, and the good things in life. Everything else is transitory. The only thing that people cannot take away from you is your character—the values that you have internalized and use to organize your life. That's what counts. It is your job to look within yourself and discover who you really are and what you are really capable of doing. When you can connect with the full potential of the spirit within you, you can build a meaningful and joyous life.

3. You recognize that your natural desires are merely a means of physical survival, and that physical survival only has meaning and purpose to the extent that it is focused upon developing character and enduring spiritual values.

We all have needs for food, sex, warmth, and clothing, and these physical necessities keep our bodies intact. But what good is it if we acquire everything in the world, lose ourselves in the process, and die a miserable death?

Take, for example, Jeremy, who worked sixty hours a week in order to succeed as an accountant with his firm. One day a senior partner (who worked much harder than Jeremy did) died. No one in the company even bothered to attend his funeral. This forced Jeremy to reconsider his values: "Do I want to kill myself to make other people rich who really don't care about me?"

A primary goal in recovery should be to become centered within yourself so you can build a foundation of enduring values. Then you can fill your life with families, jobs, associates, and possessions that have true value to you.

I've learned about this the hard way. Not many years ago, I was directing a multimillion-dollar treatment center and making an excellent salary. I had a new car and lived in a fine home. I was also a hundred pounds overweight, desperately lonely, and personally miserable. I was compulsively binging on sugar and chugging down caffeine to keep myself going. Why? Because I knew that if I had the

122

biggest and best treatment center in the world that helped alcoholics to stay sober, everything else in my life would work out. A character defect was driving me. I now call it the "messiah complex." I was psychotically devoted to everyone's well-being except my own. Many recovering people suffer from this drive.

I finally realized that I couldn't be all things to all people. Power and money are important, but must be kept in their place. I reevaluated my life and left the treatment center to open a small training and consultation firm. I had less power—but more sanity and meaning in my life.

Many recovering people sacrifice themselves because they believe that if they can help one other human being, it will make their lives worthwhile and give them meaning. This is not necessarily true. If you help other people and also work on developing yourself, you will be better people. If you help others by abandoning or sacrificing yourself to others, you will destroy yourself—and, in the long run, probably destroy everybody else around you.

People who behave in this manner in the A.A. program— those who abandon self in the effort to help others—are called "bleeding deacons." They don't "walk like they talk." They sponsor hundreds of people but are miserable themselves. They often have "white knuckle" sobriety and live in a "dry drunk." They lose themselves within the Twelve Step program. They are so caught up in trying to interpret the Steps and sharing the message with others that they forget to use the principles in their own lives. They don't recognize that A.A. is a selfish program. You must help yourself before you can help anyone else. You must recover first.

In fact, there is an order of charity in the A.A. program. Love yourself first! Why? Because if you lose yourself in sobriety, you are at high risk of going back to alcohol and drugs. And if you relapse, you can't help yourself or anyone else. Once you have learned to love yourself, you can learn to love others. Charity begins at home. Learn to love yourself first and then you can learn how to love your family, friends, and work associates. From there, you can move on out into the community and the world.

If you violate that principle of having a "first things first" selfish program, you will soon be in trouble. You must recognize that these natural desires, such as sex, food, and recreation, are not the most important things in the world. They are not worth dying for.

Then comes a frightening realization. If that stuff is not worth dying for, what is? Is there anything worth dying for? When I asked an A.A. friend about this, he suggested, "Terry, why don't you think about it another way? Is there anything that's truly worth living for?"

In my view, this is a necessary decision to make in working Step Seven. You must decide what you have—or need to have—that is truly worth living for.

4. You recognize that you cannot live exclusively by your own individual strength and intelligence, but rather need help.

I believe that people ultimately need each other, and that they find freedom by carefully selecting the people on whom they choose to rely. Sometimes, however, you don't have the opportunity to choose because circumstances force you to trust. For example, I know I can't live without the air I breathe and that I can't have good air without businesses paying attention to pollution-control standards. Or I can't live safely if someone hits me with his automobile. I can't cross a street and stay alive unless I rely on other people to follow traffic laws. I can't earn a salary unless I rely upon my boss to pay me. And if I don't have money, I can't afford to buy food or pay my rent. These interdependent relationships are fundamental to core living issues. Recognizing this interdependence and the need for other people is at the core of changing yourself.

5. You recognize that an overreliance upon yourself and isolation from others and your Higher Power has created problems in recovery.

We are limited and fallible human beings. We cannot do all things alone. To survive in the world requires cooperation. Chemical addictions rob people of their ability to cooperate. They become grandiose because the booze and drugs create the feeling that they can do all things. They become self-centered because the booze and drugs create the illusion that they don't need anything except more booze and drugs.

When most alcoholics sober up, they find themselves totally and utterly alone. The one thing that they formerly relied upon to make their lives work—the booze and drugs—doesn't work anymore. There is a hopeless feeling that nothing is left. As they sober up and their minds begin to clear, they become aware of the wreckage that they have created, and with this awareness comes shame, guilt, and nagging pain. They don't want to think about it, and above all they don't want to talk about it. So they tend to get busy, all by themselves, to try to fix it. In their isolation, they often make mistakes and end up making things worse instead of better.

It is important to inventory your need to go it alone and to examine the consequences of this approach. All things are possible with the help of other people and your Higher Power. The problem is that many people are unwilling or unable to accept help, especially when it comes to dealing with their own character defects.

In A.A., recognizing the need for help is often called "surrendering." I don't believe that surrendering means giving up responsibility. Surrendering does not mean that your Higher Power or other people will do all your changing for you. I believe people were created to be interdependent, to have a healthy mixture of taking responsibility and surrendering to cooperation. Independence and cooperation must form a dynamic balance.

In order to balance independence and cooperation, you need the serenity to accept the things that you can't handle, and the willingness to turn those things over to somebody or something else to take care of them. Then you need the courage to put your time and energy into things you can handle that can make a difference.

6. You recognize that you cannot live a meaningful life without humility—the true knowledge of who you are, including both your strengths and your weaknesses.

Humility doesn't mean putting yourself down. It means knowing at the core of your being who you really are. It means owning your strengths and weaknesses and truly believing that you are okay.

Humility is knowing that you have the capacity to do everything you need to do to survive. You may not be capable alone, but you have a Higher Power and other people who will help you. Humility is a tool to become free from the addictive self. It is only through self-knowledge that you can overcome the addictive tendencies you carry within you.

I don't believe people ever become totally free of themselves, nor can they transcend all of their human limitations. But you can be free to search out your true selves and actualize the real selves—that part of you that has been buried by your addiction. As a result, you can transcend your current limitations and find the means to achieve true freedom and peace of mind. You can honestly say, "I know who I am and I am enough. I no longer have to struggle with hopeless causes."

7. You regularly ask the God of your understanding to remove the defects of character that block you from practicing true humility and acting in accordance with who you really are.

By asking regularly for the removal of your character defects, you get in the habit of focusing upon your goal for personal change. On a daily basis, you remind yourself of the character defects that are causing problems in recovery, and you focus your mind upon changing or finding release from these defects. Since your character defects are deeply embedded in your personality, they usually do not disappear suddenly. You get free from them for a while and then they come back. A daily discipline is required to create an awareness of the defects and to keep you focused upon the goal of change.

A prayer I recommend is: "God give me the courage and strength to know who I really am, to act accordingly in my life, and to refrain from diverting my time, energy, and interest into my character defects." In addition to praying, however, you still must do the legwork. You have to stop acting out the defects and begin doing something else instead. You have to actualize the sober life. You have to make the principles of the program real in the practice of your life. And in doing that, your Higher Power takes away your defects.

POINTS TO REMEMBER

In completing Step Seven you:

1. Regularly examine your goals in life and what you are doing to achieve them.
2. Recognize that character building (psychological growth) and the development of spiritual values are the only meaningful and enduring goals in life.
3. Recognize that your natural desires are merely a means of physical survival, and that physical survival only has meaning and purpose to the extent that it is focused upon developing character and enduring spiritual values.
4. Recognize that you could not live exclusively by your own individual strength and intelligence, but rather need help.
5. Recognize that an overreliance upon self and isolation from others and your Higher Power has created problems in recovery.
6. Recognize that you cannot live a meaningful life without humility—the true knowledge of who you are, including both your strengths and your weaknesses.
7. Regularly ask the God of your understanding to remove the defects of character that block you from practicing true humility and acting in accordance with who you really are.

12

IDENTIFYING THOSE WE HAVE HARMED

The first seven Steps involve internal change. Starting with Step Eight, you have to begin repairing the things around you that were damaged by your addiction. Steps Eight and Nine tell you that in order to repair the damage, you must make a list of all the people you have harmed and become willing to make amends to them all.

Making amends doesn't mean you say a shallow "I'm sorry." It means you make an honest attempt to fix what you have broken. In order to make amends, you must acknowledge that you have hurt others, that you are sorry about what you have done, and that you are willing to do what is necessary to put things right. If you stole something, you pay it back. If you damaged something, you do whatever is in your power to fix it. That's what making amends means.

Step Eight is one of the most concrete and specific of all the Twelve Steps and one of the easiest to understand.

There is no question in my mind what this Step tells recovering people to do.

1. You make a list of all the people who were harmed by your addiction.

The key question is: "Who has been hurt by my addiction?" Notice that at this point you are not asking, "Who has hurt me?" In early recovery it is tempting to focus upon how others have hurt you and to become hypnotized by your own pain. In this way, you can use the behavior of others to justify your own. "Since you hurt me, I have the right to hurt you back!" "Since you won't make amends to me, I don't have to make amends to you!" The issue here is not about keeping score. Rather, the point is to find out what you have done to hurt others so you can repair the damage and be free from it.

It's far more difficult to think about whom you have harmed than it is to blame others. Usually most of the harm has been done to people you love, which makes it even harder. "Why do I need to dig around in the past?" you ask yourself. "I can't change the past, so why bother to think about it?" The problem is that the past will continue to haunt you for as long as you refuse to face the damage you have caused to others and do not try your best to fix it. You must face the past so that you can get free from it. You find this freedom by paying the price necessary to make the needed repairs.

Make a list (write it down) of all the persons you have harmed in any way. Ouch! "You mean I have to dig up all this wreckage from my past and review it?" Yes, that is exactly what this Step says to do. You have to identify who you hurt, and what you did to hurt them, and then you have to write it down.

130

I recommend that people take a sheet of paper and divide it into three columns. In the first column, list all the people you have harmed. In the second column, list what you did that harmed them. Then, in the third column, write down what you think you need to do to make amends.

It is important to be as specific as you can. John started an Eighth Step by writing, "I hurt women by leading them on and then rejecting them." His sponsor pointed out that this was too vague and general to be helpful. "What women did you hurt and how exactly did you hurt them?" his sponsor asked. "Most important, what did that hurt have to do with your addiction?"

John rewrote that part of his Eighth Step like this: "Who did I hurt? My girlfriend named Jenny. What did I do to hurt her? When I got fired for drinking on the job, I told her that I loved her when I really didn't in order to manipulate her into letting me live with her until I could find another job. As soon as I got another job, I moved out and broke off the relationship. What did this have to do with my addiction? At the time, I was desperate and scared to death because I was out of control of my drinking and drugging. I felt if I were honest, she wouldn't have helped me. If I had not been addicted, I wouldn't have been fired in the first place and I would not have felt a need to lie in order to get help."

2. You identify what needs to be done to repair the damage.

Amends simply means "to mend," to fix, or to make better. You have to fix the damage you caused wherever possible. But in Step Eight you are not fixing it. You are just becoming aware of what needs fixing, and what it will take to make repairs. When John was thinking about what he needed to do to fix the damage he had done to Jenny, he wrote, "I need to call her up and apologize for what I did. I also need to repay her for the three months of rent and food expenses that she provided."

3. You make a list of all the persons who have harmed you.

In the book *Twelve Steps and Twelve Traditions* (the Twelve and Twelve), you are told to make a second list, this time with the names of the people who have harmed you. You need to ask, "Who hurt me and what did they do?"

You identify the people who have hurt you so that you will be able to forgive them. That's right. You must become willing to let others off the hook. You must say, "Yes, you hurt me, but that is okay. I can let that go." You forgive others so that you can get free of the blaming and resentment that you often feel. When locked into blaming others, you can distract yourself from the true work involved in Steps Seven and Eight—repairing the harm you have done to others.

4. You forgive the people who have hurt you.

You forgive them. You let them off the hook. You psychologically acknowledge to yourself, "It's okay. I'm not going to hold this person responsible for this wrong." The word *forgive* is a combination of two words—*for* and *give*. I think about forgiving as "giving before the fact." You forgive the person for the wrongs they committed against you. You give them total absolution for what they did to you before they ever ask for it. That's forgiveness. You say, "Yes, you hurt me and it was very painful, but I now hold you harmless for that."

You don't forgive other people in order to help them; you do it to help yourself. When you have been injured, you only have two choices—you can forgive or you can resent. *Resentment* is an interesting word. It comes from the root *send*, which means "to be taken from one place to another." *Re* means "to do over again." When you resent something, you send the same message of anger to yourself over and over again. Recycling the anger causes stress and stress causes new pain and problems. The new pain and problems feed your resentment, and so the cycle continues until you drive yourself crazy. And when you get crazy enough, you drink over it.

In my understanding, the Twelve Step program has nothing against the emotion of anger, but the program has everything against the process of resentment. Resentment is recycled anger. It is unresolved anger that grows in its power to cause you anguish. The anger amplifies, intensifies, and magnifies over time until it destroys you—and the antidote is forgiveness.

People often ask me to explain this concept. How is it that one forgives another? It's different for everyone, but there are a couple of exercises I suggest that people try. First, you write down what the person did that harmed you. Then you write them a letter telling them exactly what you believe they did that hurt you. You are not going to mail this letter, but you write it.

Next, you write down exactly how you felt about it at the time and exactly how you feel about it now. Then you write that you love them, that you care about them, and you forgive what they did that hurt you. You tell them it's okay now, and you no longer hold them responsible. You no longer hold them in bondage to do anything about it.

Finally, you write in this letter, "I am big enough and capable enough to handle what you did to me." That's what forgiveness implies. It implies a foundation of strength that is big enough, strong enough, and capable enough to handle adversity from another without crumbling or seeking revenge.

Resentment is misdirected revenge. Alcoholics take revenge against others by destroying themselves. The classic
saying that describes resentment is "cutting off your nose to
spite your face." Another illustration of this is the story
about a man who comes home and finds his wife in bed
with a lover. The husband picks up a gun and points it at his
own head. When the wife laughs at this, he glares at her and
says, "Go ahead and laugh, you're next!"

That's what resentment does to you. You're mad at
somebody else and you put a gun to your own head and
blow your own brains out. That's why you must forgive
those who have harmed you. You can't ask to be forgiven
by somebody else until you have cleaned your own house
by forgiving others.

**5. You examine the consequences of making amends to
discover when doing so would further harm you or others.**

Amends means fixing and restitution means you give back.
But before you make amends, you have to examine the
consequences of making those amends. Why? Because
sometimes you can make things worse by trying to fix them.

John had an affair with a married woman while he was
drinking. She got pregnant, broke off the affair, and let her
husband believe that the child was his. Six years later, when
John got sober, he realized he had a wonderful little daughter who didn't know that he was her father. John knew that
he had wronged the woman and the girl. So what should he
do now? Should he tell the daughter, or the mother, or the
husband about what he did? John decided against it. He
believed he would cause more harm by trying to make
amends openly.

You are to make amends *except* where doing so would
harm others. So you think about the consequences of the
amends that you need to make before you act on them

irresponsibly. Father Martin is very clear about what a sober life is. Sober people plan before they execute and evaluate when they are done. When using a sober problem-solving style, you plan, act, and evaluate. When using an addictive style, you overreact, regret, and blame others. Both are simple formulas. You must consider what formula you are using before you take Step Nine. Are you overreacting? Are you regretting what you did and blaming somebody else? Or are you planning before you act, acting, and then evaluating what you did?

A written Step Eight can be a valuable tool in helping you to see how you are conducting your life sober. You have to figure out exactly what you need to do to fix the damage you caused. In Step Eight, you don't actually do it. You just get ready.

Many of the Steps require a two-part process. First, you get ready, and then you act. In Steps Two and Three, you get ready to believe; then you come to believe. You prepare to let others know who you are; then you share yourself openly. In Steps Four and Five, you get ready to clean house spiritually; then you do it. In Step Eight, you get ready to make amends, and in Step Nine, you actually do it.

There is a saying "God writes us messages in the consequences of our behavior." You look at your past history to learn from it. History teaches that if you refuse to learn from your mistakes, you are condemned to repeat them, or "history repeats itself." If you refuse to consciously acknowledge those you have hurt and what you did that hurt them, you are condemned to hurt others in the same way.

At the start you say, "Sobriety is just one awful thing after another!" Then, when you get into recovery and start resolving some things once and for all, you find it's not one thing after another. It's the same thing over and over again! And you will continue to recycle the same problems over and over again until you break out of this trap by doing two things: First, you identify the people you have harmed and make amends to them, and second, you identify the people who have hurt you and forgive them.

These two keys form a trick lock that opens the door to a meaningful sobriety. It's like a nuclear missile silo. In order to launch the missile, you have to turn two keys at the same time. The problem is that they are so far apart that you can't turn both of them by yourself. You have to have help. You need to have someone to hold onto one of the keys and then, together, you turn them both at once. Why? Because this is a cycle. I can't forgive myself until I forgive others, and I can't forgive others until I can forgive myself.

POINTS TO REMEMBER

In completing Step Eight you:

1. Make a list of all the people harmed by your addiction.
2. Identify what needs to be done to repair the damage.
3. Make a list of all the persons who have harmed you.
4. Forgive the people who have hurt you.
5. Examine the consequences of making amends to discover when doing so would further harm you or others.

13

MAKING AMENDS

STEP NINE
Made direct amends to such people wherever possible, except when to do so would injure them or others.

Step Nine tells people in recovery to make direct amends to others except when to do so would injure them or others. Notice that it doesn't say, "when to do so would injure me." The primary goal of making amends is not to feel better about yourself. It is to repair the damage caused by your addiction and to repay the debts that you owe to the people you have hurt.

There is no such thing as a "free lunch" in life. Either you will pay now or you'll pay later, with interest. Psychologically, the interest you pay is guilt and shame. Until you repair past damage, it eats away at your insides. Not only do you figure out what you broke and what you have to do to fix it, you also fix it.

You don't have to make amends. If you have unfinished business from your addiction, you have three choices: You can make amends and try to repair the relationship; you can lie to yourself and pretend that it isn't a problem; or you can end the relationship by acknowledging that the damage is too severe to fix and letting it go. It's important to think seriously before ending relationships. Amends may be difficult, but the process often works in saving valuable relationships. However, if you do your best to try to fix it and you can't, you need to turn it over and let it go. You don't have to live with it the rest of your life. You can pay the price to be done with it.

The wreckage of your addictive past is like a pile of garbage in your backyard. You can choose to live with it, you can pretend it isn't there, or you can hire someone to haul it away. Each approach carries a price. In the long run, it is less expensive to clean up the mess and to haul it away once and for all. You pay the price once. You don't keep paying later with interest. The longer you put it off, the more interest you owe.

People can get into serious trouble trying to make amends before thoroughly completing the first six Steps. Suppose you did only a superficial Step Four; you lied, conned, and hustled through Step Five; and then you rationalized Steps Six and Seven. When you went through Steps Eight and Nine, you would walk away from the process empty. You would not be healed. Instead, you would feel shattered and resentful. That's why these Steps are in order. And that's why you are told to be fearless and thorough from the very start: "Rarely have we seen a person fail who has thoroughly followed our path." Thoroughly following the path means working each Step thoroughly to the best of your ability in the correct order.

You don't make amends simply to avoid pain. The goal is to pay the price necessary to get free of the past so you can live to your fullest capacity. It takes courage to work the amends Steps. It is hard work. But it is worth it. If you don't face the wreckage of the past and clean it up, you die a little bit every day. If you face the past and deal with it, you can put it behind you once and for all.

If you choose to make amends, the recommendations that follow may be helpful.

1. You develop a strong sobriety program that will allow you to maintain sobriety while making amends to others.

Making amends can be difficult because you can never be sure what is going to happen. Sometimes people will accept your amends and at other times they won't. When others refuse to accept your amends, it can be painful, and, if you don't have a strong sobriety program, you can return to alcohol and drugs to cope with the pain. Thus, it is important to have a strong enough recovery program so that making amends won't cause relapse.

Before making amends, it is a good idea to have thoroughly completed the first seven Steps. Remember that Bill Wilson numbered the Steps when he wrote them down, implying that they were meant to be worked in a specific order. Each Step leads you into a level of personal growth that is necessary for the successful completion of the next Step. Before leaping into making amends, be sure that you have made the necessary internal changes in attitude to ensure that you will be able to make amends without either making things worse or relapsing.

Regular attendance at a home group is helpful when working the amends Steps. Making amends can be stressful, and you need to be tied into a group of people who know you well and can provide reality testing and support. It is also important to have an active relationship with a sponsor who has already completed the amends Steps. By "active" I mean that you talk with your sponsor at least three times a week over the phone, see him or her at a meeting at least once a week, and talk in face-to-face conversation at least once a week. With this type of active recovery program, you should be able to handle anything that comes up.

Just to show what can happen when making amends, let's look at an example. Gail had been sober about nine months. She felt guilty because her addiction really hurt her ex-husband, Don. He had finally divorced her after she refused to go to A.A. or to stay sober after her third treatment. She realized that she needed to make amends, so she set up an appointment to talk with him.

During the conversation, Gail told Don that she was an alcoholic and that she was sorry for all that her alcoholism had caused him. Don got a cold look in his eyes and said, "I don't care if you're sorry or not. I hate your guts and I don't want to see you anymore. Get out of my life and stay out! I don't forgive you. I don't think what you did is okay and I don't want you to say you're sorry. Go put salve on your guilt somewhere else!" He then threw her out of the office.

Gail was badly shaken by the experience. She left the office holding back her tears and immediately called her sponsor. They had dinner and talked long into the night. The next evening, she went to her home group and shared the story with them.

By talking about the experience, Gail learned an important lesson about making amends—you don't make amends to obtain forgiveness. When you make amends, you try to the best of your ability to repair broken relationships. And sometimes the damage is so severe that it cannot be repaired. But this doesn't mean that making amends didn't work. After making amends, Gail felt free of her ex-husband for the first time in her life. She could now let go emotionally and stop punishing herself for what had happened. The amends process will either fix a relationship or end it. This is what making amends is all about—paying the price to get free from the past once and for all.

2. You plan when and how to make amends to each person in an effective manner.

Since making amends is a serious and difficult process, it is best not to rush into it unprepared. It is not a good idea to pick up the phone impulsively, call seventeen people in one day, and blurt out, "I'm sorry!" It is important to create a plan. Take the list of people that you developed in Step Eight and decide the order in which you will make amends. Decide what you are going to say and review it with your sponsor. Then make appointments to talk with each one. Spread out the appointments to make sure you have time to recuperate from the stress of each encounter. Remember that one of the goals of making amends is for you to heal on the inside. This takes time and the willingness to talk about the thoughts and feelings that surfaced during each amends session. The amends process is a growth experience. It's a freeing process, and you need to have quiet time after each experience to listen to what is happening inside of you.

3. You approach the amends process with an attitude of quiet sincerity.

A recovering alcoholic named Bill was eager to make amends. Even though he hadn't completed his Fourth and Fifth Steps, he felt a need to put the past behind him. Against the advice of his sponsor, he impulsively went to make amends to his wife. He was scared to death and still privately resented her for divorcing him because of his drinking.

When Bill sat down with his wife, he froze up and couldn't think of what to say.

"Well, what do you want to talk to me about?" his wife asked.

Without thinking, Bill blurted out, "Dammit, I'm sorry for what happened and I want us to get back together!" There was anger in his voice. The conversation quickly degenerated into an argument and created more pain and problems.

Bill wasn't ready to make amends. He hadn't worked out the resentment he felt toward his wife, nor had he identified his controlling and demanding nature as a character defect. As a result, his character defects created an atmosphere that prevented him from making amends.

In order for amends to work, you need to have grown sufficiently in recovery to be able to adopt an attitude of quiet sincerity. You need to mean what you say and have resolved your anger and blaming so that you can feel and express true sorrow and regret over what you have done.

4. You start making amends by admitting the reality of your addiction and the problems it has caused.

You make amends by preparing what you are going to say and making an appointment. In making the appointment, you can say something like this: "I need to see you to discuss something important. Would you be willing to meet with me for fifteen or twenty minutes when it is convenient?"

When you meet with the person, a good way to begin is by acknowledging your addiction and the pain and problems it has caused. You can say, "I'm now in recovery from chemical dependence. I've been sober for six months. When we knew each other, I was chemically dependent but I didn't know it. Looking back now, I can see that I was out of control and I did things that hurt you. At the time, I was not aware of how it was hurting you. Now I know that it did. I was out of control then and you need to know that. You also need to know that I'm still responsible for it. And I'm sorry. I deeply regret hurting you."

What does it mean to "regret"? It means that if you could relive your life, you would do it differently. But you realize that some things in life can't be done over again. That's a regret. A regret is a sincere belief that if you had the power to go back in time, you would behave differently. And you have to tell the person that.

If you are making amends to your son, you might say something like this: "If I could go back in time and relive the period of your childhood, I wouldn't get drunk and beat you." In making amends to your wife, you might say, "If I could relive the first four years of our marriage, I wouldn't get drunk and go out and have affairs." To your boss, you might say, "If I had it to do over again, I wouldn't steal from you. I did that because I was into addictive insanity. I wouldn't do it now. If I could go back and do it again, I would behave differently."

No matter whom you make amends to, it is important to say that you are in recovery, want to repair past damage, and are committed to living a different kind of life. You could say it like this: "I know that I've caused pain and problems in the past. I'm sober and in recovery now and regret what I've done. I'd like to repair the damage to our relationship if that is possible. So here is the money I stole from you, with interest. Here is payment for the property I damaged. I can never pay back the emotional harm I caused you, and I know that. But I just want you to know that I'm sorry. And I want to know what I can do, within reason and within my capacity, to fix it."

This is a powerful process if approached with quiet sincerity and humility. Sincerity means that you mean what you say. Humility means that you know exactly who you are, and exactly why you did what you did. By knowing exactly where you stand today and what you can and cannot do to repair the damage of your past behaviors, you can make amends. You can fix it or end it.

The final task of making amends is actually paying back what you owe.

5. You complete the amends process by paying or making promises to pay whatever obligations are owed.

Making amends means you fix what you broke. Sometimes the damage is emotional and all you can do is to apologize and communicate your regrets by saying that if you could relive the past, you wouldn't do it that way. It helps those whom you hurt when they hear you admit your role in the problems. One man made amends to his wife by saying, "When we were married, my drinking made the last three years of our marriage a hell on earth. I put you through a lot of pain and it wasn't your fault. It was my fault. I know that now, and I own it. And I hope you are not punishing yourself for it, because I did it to you. You didn't do it." This was a powerful healing experience for both the alcoholic and his wife.

And if the damaged person isn't in Al-Anon and replies, "Oh, no. It really wasn't your fault. You must understand that I ... blah. ..." Well, you have to be prepared for that too.

Making amends can produce a sense of peace and well-being. You can leave the experience feeling more together as a person. Your shame and guilt can diminish and the nagging pain can disappear. Making amends can help you to feel centered, as if you have an anchor or a foundation in life.

You now know who you are in your strengths and your weaknesses. You know where you stand in life. You know what's yours and what's not yours. You know what you have a right to and what you don't. And when you have something that you have a right to, something that you have earned legitimately, there isn't anyone who can take it away. And if you have realigned your values to realize that the most important things you can possess are psychological and spiritual capacities and maturity, then, finally, you're free!

POINTS TO REMEMBER

In completing Step Nine you:

1. Develop a strong sobriety program that allows you to maintain sobriety while making amends to others.
2. Develop a plan for when and how to make amends to each person in an effective manner, and review it with your sponsor.
3. Prepare to approach the amends process with an attitude of quiet sincerity.
4. Start making amends by admitting the reality of your addiction and the problems it has caused.
5. Become willing to complete the amends process by paying or making promises to pay whatever obligations are owed.

=14=

DAILY REVIEW

As a result of Steps One through Seven, you have fixed yourself on the inside. Through Steps Eight and Nine, you have fixed what you can fix on the outside. Now that your lives are back in working order, Step Ten tells you to watch yourself carefully. When you do something that's harmful to your recovery, you fix it immediately. You correct your mistakes as soon as you become aware of them. The Steps acknowledge that you do not seek perfection in this. You seek progress but not perfection.

The Tenth Step helps you monitor your progress by catching mistakes early and correcting them before they grow into major problems.

There are six specific tasks that need to be addressed in ongoing Tenth Step work.

1. You develop a format for completing a daily inventory that reviews both your strengths and your weaknesses.

In order to complete a daily inventory, you must have a system for reviewing your thoughts, feelings, and behaviors

147

that will help you determine whether you have healthy, sobriety-centered responses or have fallen back into self-defeating addictive responses. It helps to use a questionnaire or checklist that provides something to think about, something to which you can compare yourself.

There are many such "daily inventory" formats available for this purpose. Many people use one of the many daily meditation books available through the Hazelden Foundation. In the *Staying Sober Workbook*, for example, there are morning and evening inventory forms developed for relapse-prone people that can be adapted easily for working Step Ten.

I recommend that people do two inventories every day—one in the morning and one in the evening. In your morning inventory, you plan your day. The key questions are: "What do I need to do today to maintain my recovery and keep growing?" and "What do I need to do today to meet my obligations and responsibilities in life?" In the evening inventory, you review your progress. Here the questions are a little different: "What have I done well today?" "What have I done poorly?" "What do I need to do about it?" "Are there any warning signs popping up to tell me I'm in trouble in my recovery?"

Once you have a daily inventory format, you can proceed.

2. You make a commitment to practice this inventory on a daily basis so that it will become a habitual part of your life.

Some people ask, "How long do we have to keep taking this daily inventory?" My answer is: "Until it becomes so comfortable to you that you don't want to stop." Do only recovering people need daily inventories? No. Many successful people do daily inventories. They plan in the morn-

148

ing and review in the evening. Also, many people who have achieved greatness have kept a daily journal.

There seems to be a relationship between success and doing daily inventories and journaling. Most successful people do both. Most people who regard their lives as failures do neither. I believe that doing inventories and keeping a journal create greatness in people. By confronting yourself on paper every day, you are forced to consciously examine your decisions and reactions. This gives you the opportunity to reach for greatness.

Why is it that many people don't keep journals? Many people just are not comfortable with writing. Others are afraid to put their thoughts on paper. But it is helpful to learn how to do it, because writing about your day-to-day thoughts is the best way to "sort out your head." The written inventories don't have to be perfect. Remember, the goal is to sort out your thinking so you can catch irrational or addictive thoughts before they create serious problems.

Many people find that when they are doing well, they have no problem keeping a daily journal. As problems begin to develop, it becomes more difficult to find time to write. I don't believe this is an accident—this kind of avoidance is a psychological defense. People don't want to confront themselves with the reality of thoughts and behaviors, so they make excuses to stop doing their daily inventory.

3. You recognize your personal strengths and weaknesses as they become apparent in your daily life.

If you are to recover, you must learn to judge the quality of your thoughts and actions. To do this, you need an objective standard that reflects high ideals. Many recovering people use their personal interpretation of the Twelve Step principles as a guide.

I have boiled down my understanding of the basic principles of A.A. into three simple mandates and injunctions. The mandates tell people what they need in order to have a comfortable sobriety. The injunctions tell them what they need to avoid.

In my mind, the Twelve Step program mandates three things—rigorous honesty, earning your keep, and respect for the rights of others. "Rigorous honesty" means that you tell the truth. "Earning your keep" means that you stop expecting something for nothing and become willing to pay a fair price for what you receive. "Respect for the rights of others" means that you live and let live. You allow others to freely pursue their own happiness and recovery without interference.

I also believe the Twelve Step program tells people not to do three things—don't lie, don't cheat, and don't steal. Lying is telling others that something is not true when you know that it is. Cheating is trying to get something by deception that you haven't earned and therefore don't deserve. Stealing is taking something by force, something that is not yours.

In recovery you stop lying to yourself and others. You strive to practice rigorous honesty. You stop cheating yourself and others. You only take from life what you have earned and stop trying to con people into giving you things that you haven't earned and don't deserve. And you stop stealing. You stop trying to take by force things that are not rightfully yours. Stealing can involve more than the taking of physical possessions. You can steal someone's reputation through malicious gossip, or their time by being chronically late for appointments. You may rob your children of trust by failing to keep a promise you've made to them or of joy by punishing or blaming them unfairly.

Twelve Step principles teach people that the only way to

have things that are truly theirs is to earn them through responsible actions. Then those things are theirs to keep, to share, and to do with what they want because they have earned them. They apply these fundamental principles as the external standard to judge themselves. And they ask for the help and feedback of other people.

4. You utilize a personal journal to document the developing pattern of strengths and weaknesses in your life.

Recovering people don't just *keep* journals; they periodically read them. By reading several months of entries in one sitting, they can take stock of their progress over time. They can see if they are growing in the long run or if they are slowly slipping back into addictive thinking and life unmanageability.

5. You make conscious efforts to utilize your strengths in providing service to others.

Sober people use their strengths to help others, and in doing this, they build their own strengths further. It is important to remember that you were given your strengths for a reason. You have a purpose. There is something for you to do with your life. Sober people tend to seek out the meaning and purpose of their lives. They find a way to use their strengths to benefit themselves and contribute to the world.

When I am dying, I want to be able to look back upon my life and know that my life has made a difference. I want to see that I have cut a path of love and positive contributions. I want the world to be a better place because I have passed this way.

We all have an impact upon our personal world. On a day-to-day basis, we make it either a little bit better or a little bit worse. Greatness or failure in life is not built in single dramatic events. It is built slowly and quietly, one

151

day at a time. It is the small daily decisions that prepare us for the culminating events of greatness or tragedy. We all live slowly, one day at a time, one decision at a time, one action at a time. You can choose to direct those actions toward building a better world through service to others or toward diminishing the world by retreating back into self-defeating addictive behaviors and becoming part of the world's problems. It is through your daily inventory that you learn to see what you are doing and learn how to change.

6. You make conscious efforts to admit your weaknesses and take actions to improve in those areas.

Sober people take action and get the help of others to improve in their weak areas. When they're wrong, they admit it promptly. Does this mean they're free of problems? No. It means they now have the tools to cope with the problems they have.

Psychologist Nathaniel Branden says, "Mental health is the process of trading in one set of problems for a better set of problems." You can adapt that saying to recovery from chemical dependency by saying that recovery is the process of trading in one set of problems for a better set of problems.

Steps One, Two, and Three address the problems surrounding powerlessness over alcohol and drugs. You trade these in for the problems of Steps Four and Five when you identify and share your character defects. Then you trade these in for the problems of Steps Six and Seven, actually changing your character defects by rebuilding yourself from the inside out. After that, you trade up to the problems of Steps Eight and Nine and repair damage done to others and your lifestyle. In Step Ten, you take on the problem of maintaining your serenity and peace of mind.

In my view, you work all of the Steps a little bit all of the time. But most people who succeed with the Twelve Step program put their primary focus on one Step at a time. In Step One, your primary focus is powerlessness. In Step Two, it is finding a source of help, and in Step Three you focus on following directions from that source of help. You develop a recovery program that will give you a foundation from which to work the Steps that follow.

In Step Four, your primary focus is on examining yourself and learning who you really are in your strengths and your weaknesses. In Step Five, you learn that you will still be loved and cared about even when other human beings know who you are and are not in the totality of your being.

In Step Six, you focus on getting ready to give up the character defects that are causing you pain in sobriety. You get ready to give up your crazy behavior and your alcoholic addictive thinking. In Step Seven, you focus on doing what you need to do to change. You pursue getting the courage and the strength from a power greater than yourself to do what you need to do to give up your self-defeating behaviors.

In Step Eight, your focus is listing the people you have harmed, stating very clearly what you did to hurt them, what you need to do to make amends, and becoming willing to do it. You focus on gaining the insight, courage, and strength to repair damage you have caused. In Step Nine, you fix whatever it is you damaged; that's your primary focus.

Then, during Step Ten, you focus on getting into the habit of living a comfortable, problem-free life without setting yourself up to fail before you embark on the primary work of Step Eleven.

In the Tenth Step, the primary focus is to plan your day, live responsibly, and evaluate it when you're done until you're in the habit of responsible living and feeling good about that. And this isn't easy. You can never underestimate the power of recovering chemically dependent persons to sabotage themselves, or the power of their compulsion to do so.

You are never problem-free. But by the time you are through the Steps the first time, you are able to deal responsibly with your problems in a sober state of mind, while maintaining serenity, acceptance, and knowledge of what you feel and what you think. By getting clear from the past and relatively safe from repeating it, you become able to cope, to move ahead, and to find meaning and purpose in life.

The next Step on your journey is growth.

POINTS TO REMEMBER

In completing Step Ten you:

1. Develop a format for completing a daily inventory that reviews both your strengths and your weaknesses.
2. Become committed to practice this inventory on a daily basis so that it becomes a habitual part of your life.
3. Recognize your strengths and weaknesses as they become apparent in your daily life.
4. Utilize a personal journal to document the developing pattern of strengths and weaknesses in your life.
5. Make conscious efforts to utilize your strengths in providing service to others.
6. Make conscious efforts to admit your weaknesses and take actions to improve in those areas.

15

GROWTH

<table>
<tr><td>

STEP ELEVEN

Sought through prayer and meditation to improve our conscious contact with God *as we understood Him*, praying only for knowledge of His will for us and the power to carry that out.

</td></tr>
</table>

Step Eleven is the "spiritual Step," where you improve your spiritual understanding of God. Steps One through Ten prepare you for this Step. In the first three Steps, you came to believe in a Higher Power, unconditionally, just to get sober. Most people find that the Higher Power that they come to know and understand in Step Eleven is much different from the Higher Power to which they turned in Step One.

Father Joseph Martin puts it very simply and eloquently when he says, "You can't feed spiritual steak to spiritual infants. They strangle on it." If you start talking spiritual, mystical God-concepts to alcoholics too soon in their recovery, they may very well walk out and never come back.

In the first three Steps, you must decide, "What or who is my Higher Power? What source of help is there that's bigger and stronger than I?" You identify what that is for you, although it doesn't have to be a spiritual being.

Step Eleven includes the tasks that follow.

1. You make a decision to believe in a Higher Power and to call that Higher Power God.

I had trouble understanding Step Eleven for a long time. What helped to explain it was reading the Big Book of Overeaters Anonymous, *Compulsive Overeater*, written by Bill B. In talking about finding a Higher Power, Bill explains what his sponsor told him to do. When Bill told his sponsor he didn't believe in God, his sponsor asked him, "Are you willing to believe there might be a God?" When Bill said he wasn't sure, his sponsor put it another way and asked him, "Are you open to the possibility that maybe a God exists?" To this Bill replied, "Sure! I'm willing to accept that God might exist." Then his sponsor said, "I want you to take a sheet of paper and write a description of what you would like God to be if there were a God. You don't have to say that He or She exists; just imagine that if God did exist, and you had the power to create God according to whatever you wanted Him or Her to be, what qualities or attributes would your God have?" Bill wrote out his list and entertained the possibility that maybe a God did exist, and you can too.

I believe everyone has a God—we just call God by different names. An atheist once told me, "Terry, I'm an atheist. I don't have a God." I asked him, "What do you believe in that organizes your life?"

"I believe in science," was his reply.

So his "God" was science. How do I know? Because he organized his life around it. I suggest that people think of the word GOD as an acronym for Good Orderly Direction. GOD can then be seen as the central value in your life

156

around which you organize everything else. It is the central value that provides order, meaning, and purpose to everything else you do.

If you organize your life around reason, your GOD is reason. If you organize it around getting drunk and throwing up, your GOD is booze. Every actively drinking addict has a GOD called alcohol or drugs. You may not want to accept that, but if you're chemically dependent and actively drinking or using drugs, what's the organizing principle of your life? What's the Higher Power upon which you live, breathe, and depend? The chemicals. If you're a compulsive overeater, your GOD is food. If you're codependent, your GOD is some other person whom you are trying to take care of and fix.

Your God is the central principle, the central value in your life. And to "worship" is simply to acknowledge that fact, publicly and privately. You worship your God whether or not you want to when you affirm to yourself, "Yes, this is my central meaning and purpose in life." What you often don't recognize is that you have the power to choose what you worship.

The next stage is to pretend that this hypothetical God does, in fact, exist; then you start communicating with Him and see what happens.

2. You make a decision to believe that it is possible to develop a personal relationship with the God of your understanding.

Some people wonder, "If I make up my concept of God, how can I develop a relationship?" The two key questions here need to be: (1) "If that God existed, would that God of my understanding be available to me?" and (2) "Does my idea of God give me a Higher Power that cares about me?" If either answer is no, you have created a "God concept"

157

that isn't going to be very helpful to you, and perhaps you need to rethink and come up with a better concept.

I don't believe it makes a lot of difference whether or not the God you envision really exists or whether it's simply a mental exercise. The best philosophical schools of thought tell us that it is impossible to prove that God exists or to prove that God does not exist.

Since alcoholics can't know for certain whether or not God exists, it is helpful to think about the issue on another level by asking, "Which has better consequences for me— believing that God exists or believing that He does not?" Many people find it helpful to believe God exists, even if He may not. What have you got to lose?

Then on a third level, you need to decide, "Just what kind of God is worthy of my belief?" And you have the power and the right to create that concept of God. You can choose. For most recovering people, this concept of God changes radically many times in the course of their re- covery.

Anyone who pursues a spiritual quest or a spiritual jour- ney tries to understand the nature of the nonphysical di- mension of the universe. You want to know, "What am I like? What's my essence? What is my soul? What is 'the spirit'? What is this psychic driving force within me?" These and other philosophical questions form the spiritual quest of Step Eleven.

As you learn more, you define and redefine what you believe. This process is called "expanding consciousness," but it's important to be cautious. Many Eastern philoso- phies hold that "expanded consciousness" means being aware of nothing at all, and that's not consciousness; that is unconsciousness.

When you become conscious of something, you "know," and you know on a variety of levels. You know intellectually and rationally. You know in your gut with your feelings and in your head through your intuition. And when you know, you can share truth as you understand it with others, and other people will "know" too. And you can feel it. It's called "the ring of truth." Human minds are designed for truth. Truth is necessary for growth and growth is necessary for sobriety.

3. You pray and meditate as an act of faith that a relationship with God can develop.

Once you make a decision to believe that communication with God is possible and that you are worthy to try to communicate, you make a stab at it. If you keep an open mind and withhold contempt prior to investigation, you recognize that a relationship with God could be a really interesting and worthwhile experience. So you decide to try it.

You can do this as an experiment. Many people, without ever trying, refuse to believe. You decide to try it. You create a solid concept of God and pray to it. Let me suggest a simplistic approach that identifies two processes—prayer and meditation. Prayer is talking to the God of your understanding. You put into words what you want the God of your understanding to do for you. You identify what you want from God. Meditation is listening for an answer, or discovering what God wants you to do for Him or Her.

Some people say that God is somewhere "out there." Other people say that God is our unconscious mind and is within us. I don't know which, if either, is right, and I am not sure it makes a difference, because in my experience the dialogue process itself is very beneficial.

In a book called *Think and Grow Rich*, Napoleon Hill recommends an exercise. He suggests that we create in our mind a panel of advisers, selecting historical figures we respect for the panel—people such as Abraham Lincoln or Martin Luther King. Each day, we call a meeting of our "advisers." We ask them a question and imagine how they would answer. In developing this answer, we try to take on momentarily the values of each adviser and imagine the answer each one would give us. There are some people who believe that in vividly imagining such a panel of advisers, we are actually creating or contacting "spirit guides." I believe they are creations of our mind and our imagination, but nonetheless, exercises such as these can be very powerful learning experiences that help us view a problem from a new and different perspective.

In creating the image of somebody you respect and imagining the advice that person would give you, you are taking on momentarily the qualities and values you believe that this person has possessed. You are, for a few moments, becoming more like them. This exercise forces you to stretch yourself and your value system. It allows you to contact parts of yourself you previously did not know existed.

There are dangers in believing that these imagined advisers are actually spirit guides. The major danger is that you take away your own power. You basically say to yourself, "I didn't create the answer; my spirit guide did. I am not responsible; my spirit guide is responsible." This can lead people to minimize the power of their own minds.

After you have defined your concept of God by creating a clear image of what you would like God to be, you try to communicate with that God. In essence, you must be willing to use prayer and meditation for this purpose. How do you do it? The Twelve and Twelve has clear recommendations for how to pray and what to pray for. You don't pray for a new Cadillac or ask God to "please do my laundry for me." That's not how it works. In A.A., you are advised to pray for "the knowledge of God's will for you and for the power or courage to carry it out"—your next challenge.

4. You focus your prayer and meditation upon receiving the knowledge of God's will for you and the courage to carry that out.

What is "knowledge of God's will"? I was raised as a Catholic and we called it a "vocation"—knowledge of what God meant for me to do with my life. Recovering people want to learn what is meant for them to do with their lives, what is their spiritual quest.

What is it that you are meant to do with your life? What are your natural talents and aptitudes? To what higher purpose or value can you make a commitment? This is the knowledge for which you pray. You pray that you may discover what you can make of your life now that you are sober. You pray to find a course of action that will integrate you, make you feel whole and complete, heal you, and allow you to grow.

I once listened to a lecture by Stephen Glenn, an expert on raising healthy children, who defined his concept of God in a very simple way. He said, "To me God, or a Higher Power, is some value, knowledge, or energy source outside of myself that gives life meaning and purpose. It is some value bigger than I am that gives my life meaning and purpose. It is something bigger than I that I know will live on beyond me and that makes life worth living."

5. You have personal experiences that confirm that your spiritual program is working.

Recovering people look for experiences that provide evidence that their spiritual program is working. They try to communicate with God and see if anything really happens. This is the test, the proof of the pudding. As Father Martin put it, "I don't care how good a cook you are. If you bake a pie, eat it, and get sick, it's a bad pie! I don't care how good something is in theory. If I try it and it doesn't work, it's a lousy theory."

Sober people try a spiritual approach to recovery and if it doesn't work, they give it up. But if they try it and something positive happens, they keep coming back. Most people who try the spiritual approach find that something happens. They experience a personal transformation. They have a spiritual experience or spiritual awakening.

6. You have changed as a result of your spiritual experiences.

The important questions that need to be asked are: "Have you changed as a result of your spiritual experiences?" "Are you somehow different?" In spiritual terms, this change often is called a "personal transformation." Many people report significant changes in how they feel about themselves and how they perceive and relate to the world as a result of working their spiritual program.

A psychologist named Abraham Maslow made it psychologically acceptable to have spiritual experiences. He researched highly functional people and discovered that most of them routinely had peak spiritual experiences. His research also showed that as people developed higher levels of self-esteem and self-actualization, the number of their spiritual experiences dramatically increased.

During spiritual experiences, you feel a unique sense of well-being. It is as if you are at peace with the universe. You feel extremely important and terribly insignificant all at the same time. You sense that you are part of something bigger than yourself and as a result, you feel serenity, a unique state of well-being. For a while, it seems all is right in the world and you are exactly where you need to be, exactly when you need to be there.

These moments of transformation are possible, and they occur in the lives of many recovering people.

7. You acknowledge to yourself and to others that you have changed as a result of your spiritual experiences.

The human mind is designed to deal with truth, and to find the truth, you must be willing to honestly share and critically evaluate your experiences in recovery. When you have a new, positive experience, you honestly acknowledge it. The same is also true if you try for a new experience and it doesn't work. You must honestly evaluate the negative outcomes as well as the positive.

This evaluation can be difficult. Most recovering people experience the spiritual component of the program in a unique and personal way. Another person's sense of spirituality will not necessarily be the same as yours. The spiritual practices that work well for him or her may not work for you. This is why rigorous honesty is so important. You need to start comparing notes and seeing what works and what doesn't. It is important to talk at meetings about your experiments with spirituality. In essence, you share your experiences as a form of evaluation when you try something you talk about. You also learn from others who have experimented with similar things. When you have enough information from your own and others' experiences, you choose what you believe to be true or not true, always reminding yourself that the "truth" must be reevaluated constantly. Your understanding of the truth changes as you grow and develop.

"Healthy" spirituality leads you to grow and develop, strengthening you in the long run of your life. Ultimately, it allows you to face death with meaning, purpose, dignity, and strength.

A friend of mine named Tom was dying of cancer. Tom was an atheist, and near the end of his life, we had several in-depth discussions about life, death, and the concept of God or Higher Power. Several months before he died, we went away for a weekend to camp in the desert. It was a time for us to say good-bye. We were sitting on top of his van at sunset watching three-wheeled bikes kick up dust in the desert dunes, and we talked about spirituality.

"Tom, you're an atheist," I began tentatively. "What's your sense of spirituality?"

"On one level, I believe there is a God, but here's the level I'm talking about." Tom looked out across the desert at the setting sun and the reflected colors on the sand. "I take a look around," he said, "and I know there's gotta be someone out there that makes sunsets better than I do. There's someone or something out there that makes trees better than I do. That's my concept of God. There's some organizing principle in the universe that organizes the world better than I'm capable of doing."

Tom became quiet for a moment and looked at me with deep and intense eyes: "Facing death is scary, but on some level I know that I fit into that order somewhere. I don't believe that I'm going to go on. I believe when I'm dead, that's it. I don't believe that there's an afterlife or that I'm going to go through a tunnel and come out the other side. I just can't find it in my heart to believe that. But I know that somehow in this bigger order of things, I was here for some kind of reason. I did the best I knew how and now I'm leaving."

Before Tom died, he asked his wife to give one message to the people who gathered at his memorial service. Tom's message to us was this: "The Steps of A.A. work and its promises come true."

If you know someone who is dying, get close to them, especially if they are in a Twelve Step program and have the maturity to talk about what they are experiencing. Tom shared his experience, strength, and hope right up until the moment he died, and through his death I gained. That's part of the program. People grow through sharing with others.

As I watched Tom die, as I watched him use the Twelve Step principles to gain the courage to face his death, I had to stop and ask, "Why wasn't he referring to Leo Buscaglia? Why wasn't he referring to a theologian or a psychologist? Why was he going back to the Steps?" I don't know the answer. I just ponder these things. I've seen more than one person in the program die, and the Steps have helped them do it with honor and dignity. They left this life with a sense of meaning and purpose.

But keep in mind that there are also destructive forms of spirituality, which may feel good in the short run but weaken people in the long run of their lives. I'm frightened by the expansion of mind-control cults that manipulate and exploit people under the guise of teaching spiritual growth. It makes little difference whether they are "scientific" cults like Dianetics or spiritual cults like many of the fundamentalist religious cults that are using the front of Christianity to control and manipulate people.

As you pursue your spiritual quest, you need to move cautiously. There are many approaches to spirituality that hurt people. I wouldn't trust any approach to spirituality that separates recovering people from the Twelve Step program. There is no legitimate spiritual or religious approach that I know of that has any objection at all to its members attending the Twelve Step fellowship of A.A. If you are considering a spiritual path that tells you to abandon A.A. and your recovery program . . . run for the nearest exit!

POINTS TO REMEMBER

In completing Step Eleven you:

1. Make a decision to believe in a Higher Power and to call that Higher Power God.
2. Make a decision to believe that it is possible to develop a personal relationship with the God of your understanding.
3. Pray and meditate as an act of faith that a relationship with God can develop.
4. Focus your prayer and meditation upon receiving the knowledge of God's will for you and the courage to carry that out.
5. Have personal experiences that confirm that your spiritual program is working.
6. Change as a result of your spiritual experiences.
7. Acknowledge to self and others that you have changed as a result of your spiritual experiences.

16

CARRYING THE MESSAGE

"Having had a spiritual awakening" means that you have undergone a change as a result of working these Steps. You are different now and thus are in a position to help other people do what you have done. It is important, though, not to jump the gun and start trying to carry the message before you have gone through positive change.

Fred is an example of what not to do. Fred had been sober about three months, but he weighed about 350 pounds and was a chain smoker. He was miserable. He was overreactive and could take someone's head off at a moment's notice. He was grandiose and self-centered. He wouldn't listen, and he consistently cut people off in mid-sentence. He was cold, harsh, and angry. He rarely expressed warmth or genuine concern for others. In short, his spiritual awakening had not yet occurred.

One day he stood up at a meeting and said, "If you want

what we got, do what we did!" Fred had such a poor program of recovery that he had little or no credibility. He was carrying the word to others before he himself had changed. Recovering people must be able to model something before they try to help others. In A.A. they say, "You gotta walk the walk before you talk the talk." You can't just talk a good game. If you do not "walk like you talk," what you say will not have very much credibility.

Remember that A.A. is a selfish program. Members help others because it helps them. They are there to help themselves first. Why? Because if they don't help themselves first, they can't help anybody else. It ties back into that first Tradition: "Our common welfare should come first." It's another of the many paradoxes of the program. If A.A. is not there to help them, sober people can't survive. But if they don't help themselves first, A.A. can't survive either.

Before you can effectively work the Twelfth Step and help others, you have to have that spiritual awakening. You have to recognize that a spiritual awakening has occurred and that it didn't happen by magic.

Here again, my rational side comes out. If spirituality is real, it is governed by laws and principles. If you learn what to do and activate those laws and principles, it will happen to you. The modeling process ensures the continuation of the program. Your sponsor models positive behavior for you, and you, in turn, model for others.

1. You recognize that a spiritual awakening has occurred as a result of practicing the previous eleven Steps.

This spiritual awakening is a radical change within yourself and how you operate in life, based on solid principles. It's not mumbo jumbo and it didn't happen to you by accident or fate. It happened because you began to understand how to use the spiritual and psychological laws necessary for change. In other words, you began using your mind properly to seek truth. You tried to expose mistaken notions about yourself, other people, and the world and refused to follow your old and destructive patterns. As a result, you changed in dramatic and fundamental ways. Having experienced this change, you continue to the next level.

2. You carry the message of hope and recovery to other suffering alcoholics.

Now you can tell all three parts of your A.A. story: what it was like, what happened, and what it's like now. What it was like: I was addicted to alcohol and drugs and my life was miserable. What happened: I recognized that I needed to pursue the sober life, which means abstinence plus fundamental internal and external changes in my life. Now, as a result of working the Twelve Step program, I have become a fundamentally different person than I was before. I became a person who no longer needs or desires to use alcohol or drugs. I became a person who can cope with life. I became a person who has found meaning and purpose in my existence. I've had a conversion, and now I'm different.

3. You provide service to others with no expectations of personal reward or compensation.

You freely share your recovery experience with others in personal conversations, by speaking at meetings, and by sponsoring newcomers. In short, you share your experience, your strength, and hope. In A.A., the slogan for this is, "In order to keep it, I have to give it away."

This process of sharing will lead you to a new period of growth. You recover by helping others and you help others by sharing what worked for you, by giving it away. To keep growing, you must keep sharing. If both of your hands are full and you don't want to let go of what you have, you

169

can't pick up anything else. When you give something away, you free up one of your hands to pick up something new.

4. You participate in the ongoing recovery process with other alcoholics by attending A.A. meetings and sharing your experience, strength, and hope.

How many meetings do you have to attend? That's up to you. Seven a week if you want. Once a month if you want. You have choices and you have the responsibility to choose for yourself. By the time you arrive at Step Twelve, you're stable in your sobriety and you're able to make choices. You can listen to the experiences of others, compare that to your own experiences, and make your own decisions. Recovery is about options. The healthier you are, the more choices you have and the better able you are to choose responsibly.

As a general guideline, it is a good idea to attend a minimum of one meeting per week to maintain your recovery. Most people choose to invest more time. When you consider that you have a fatal disease that has a tendency toward relapse, that is not a great deal of maintenance. If you had cancer, you would be willing to spend one hour each week to keep from dying. Addiction kills. One hour a week seems like a reasonable investment of time to stay alive.

5. You practice Twelve Step principles in all your affairs by bringing the spirit of love and tolerance into all aspects of your life.

You practice the principles in all of your activities. That is the bottom line of A.A. The important thing is not how many meetings you attend or how many people you sponsor. The bottom line is how well you understand and prac-

170

tice the principles. You work the Twelve Step program in your mind and heart and you act out the program in everything that you do. Once you have internalized the principles of A.A., you can move ahead in your life. You're free.

This doesn't mean you don't have any limits. It doesn't mean you don't have good days and bad days or that you don't make mistakes or do stupid things. Sometimes you may even make conscious decisions to do things that you know are not in your best interests. You are a fallible human being, so you will periodically mess things up. By working the Steps, you have learned to cope with life in a sober way, but now you also have the power to learn from the mistakes you make in sobriety.

6. You continue to grow spiritually while recognizing that you can make progress but can never achieve perfection.

Spiritual progress is the process of trading in one set of problems for a better set of problems. As you learn and grow, you trade in one concept of reality for a different concept of reality. You are designed to seek the truth, to grow, and to love. In order to survive, your primary love has to be the love of truth. To me, God is ultimate truth.

Will you ever completely "know" this truth in your life? I don't have an answer today and I may never have it. Is there an "ultimate truth"? No one can prove that there is or there isn't. I choose to believe that there is because I think there are psychological benefits in believing that "truth" exists. It certainly is better than believing that life is chaotic and meaningless. If you believe that life has meaning and purpose, you will seek after it. If you believe that life is meaningless, you will lose your motivation and lapse into depression and hopelessness.

The God of your understanding is what you create in your life, so you had better choose one and realize that your beliefs, thoughts, behaviors, and relationships all have consequences. And it all starts out on this fundamental core level—what do you believe? What you believe has consequences because it creates what you think. What you think has consequences because it creates your feelings and behaviors. What you do has consequences because it creates or destroys your relationships. And, finally, your relationships have consequences because ultimately they create or destroy the history of mankind. You are plugged into that Big Picture, and what each of you does counts. In the words of John Kennedy, "One person can make a difference, and every person should try."

When you are ready to die, the ultimate question is, "Is the world a better place because you were here?" Will your death be a tribute to the belief that there's nothing but chaos and disorder in the world or a tribute to the fact that there is meaning and purpose for us?

We are all going to die, and, to a large extent, we can choose our deaths by making careful decisions about how we live. People who live courageously die courageously. People who live violent lives tend to die violent deaths. People who surround themselves with others who love them in life tend to die surrounded by people who love them.

I once met a ninety-six-year-old woman on an airplane. Although old in years, her eyes sparkled and she projected a marvelous sense of life. "How do you stay so young?" I asked her. She replied, "We grow old as we live young." Most people seem to get old before they are thirty. And the proof of that is that a thirty-year-old can't communicate with a twenty-year-old, and it isn't the twenty-year-old's problem.

The Twelve Steps are designed to open you up to life, to teach you how to live effectively, and ultimately to give you a spiritual awakening so you can carry the message to alcoholics and practice these principles in all of your affairs.

POINTS TO REMEMBER

In completing Step Twelve you:

1. Recognize that a spiritual awakening has occurred as a result of practicing the previous eleven Steps.
2. Carry the message of hope and recovery to other suffering alcoholics.
3. Provide service to others with no expectations of personal reward or compensation.
4. Participate in the ongoing recovery process with other alcoholics by attending A.A. meetings and sharing your experience, strength, and hope.
5. Practice Twelve Step principles in all your affairs by bringing the spirit of love and tolerance into all aspects of your life.
6. Continue to grow spiritually while recognizing that you can make progress but can never achieve perfection.

17

THE PROMISES

What will happen if you thoroughly follow the path described in the Twelve Steps? Will it be worth the effort? The Big Book of Alcoholics Anonymous (pages 83 and 84) tells what you can expect after working Steps One through Nine in the form of twelve promises: (The Promises reprinted with the permission of AA World Services, Inc.)

If we are painstaking about this phase of our development, we will be amazed before we are half-way through. [1] We are going to know a new freedom and a new happiness. [2] We will not regret the past nor wish to shut the door on it. [3] We will comprehend the word serenity and [4] we will know peace. [5] No matter how far down the scale we have gone, we will see how our experience can benefit others. [6] That feeling of uselessness and self-pity will disappear. [7] We will lose interest in selfish things and gain interest in our fellows. [8] Self-seeking will slip away. [9] Our whole attitude and outlook upon life will change. [10] Fear of people and of economic insecurity will leave us. [11] We will intuitively know how to handle situations which used to baffle us. [12] We will suddenly realize that God is doing for us what we could not do for ourselves.

The first four promises deal with changes in feeling. The First Promise—"We are going to know a new freedom and of a new happiness"—deals with your ability to get free of your past, to get out of the trap of your addiction, and to have a new and happier life.

The Second Promise—"We will not regret the past nor wish to shut the door on it"—tells you you will be able to remember your past without hurting about it. You will be able to remember what has happened to you and resolve the painful memories. By telling your story and expressing the shame, guilt, and nagging pain to others, you find relief. You can tell your story without experiencing pain. You come to accept your past as a necessary part of who you are, and you come to believe at the core of your being that it is okay.

The Third Promise says "We will comprehend the word serenity." Serenity doesn't necessarily mean that you feel good at all times. Serenity is not a state of sobriety-based intoxication. Serenity is the ability to accept pleasant and unpleasant feelings; to know what you feel and to accept it even if that feeling is uncomfortable; to know that you are not your feelings; to be aware that you are bigger than your feelings, that you are the spirit or the consciousness that experiences your feelings. As a result of this knowledge, you can stop being a slave to your feelings. You will be able to stop upsetting yourself with the fact that you are a fallible human being who experiences both pleasant and unpleasant emotions. You can be content with the fact that you do make mistakes.

The Fourth Promise—"We will know peace"—is a direct result of accepting yourself. There will be periods in your life when you will know peace of mind. You will know what it feels like to be calm and relaxed. You will begin to know at a deep level that everything is the way it's supposed to be. You will be able to accept that what was, is, and make plans to move ahead from there.

In order to make the first three Promises come true, you must learn how to do three things: First, you must learn how to identify, label, and communicate your feelings; second, you must reconstruct your alcohol- and drug-use story and keep telling it to others until you can do so without feeling guilt, shame, or nagging pain; third, you must learn to accept both pleasant and unpleasant feelings as a normal and natural part of life.

The next two Promises deal with behavioral change. Addiction immobilizes. Sobriety allows you to get moving again through the process of self-actualization. "To actualize" means to make real through action. You must learn that it is not enough just to feel better. You must learn to think better and to act better.

The Fifth Promise states that "No matter how far down the scale we have gone," no matter how sick you were or how destructive your addiction was, "we will see how our experience can benefit others." You are going to be able to use your past experience in service to other people. You no longer have to say to yourself, "Isn't it awful that I had this horrible addiction?" You can now rephrase this and say, "Isn't it incredible how much I have learned by surviving my addiction?" You know that you are stronger and more capable because of your addiction than you ever could have been without it, and you are able to bring that strength with you into sobriety and use it for good.

The Sixth Promise says "That feeling of uselessness and self-pity will disappear." You can channel your newfound strength and self-confidence into your sobriety. You can become useful instead of useless. You can experience self-

177

worth instead of self-pity. In short, you can begin to feel good about who you are and what you are doing with your life.

The Seventh Promise—"We will lose interest in selfish things and gain interest in our fellows"—and the Eighth Promise—"Self-seeking will slip away"—deal with goals related to changes in relationships. When you are actively addicted, you are addictively self-centered. The world stops at the tip of your nose. Promise Seven tells you that your addictive self-centeredness is going to fade and you're going to become interested in other people. You are going to become actively involved socially. Your motives will expand to include the well-being of other people as well as your own. You will be able to become productively involved with other people.

To obtain these Promises, you need to acquire a healthy social awareness and to recognize that it's in your best interests to develop healthy, loving, and caring relationships with other people. Not only do you have to take care of yourself, you also need to learn to care for others.

The last four Promises deal with a fundamental change in your world view. In the Ninth Promise, you are told that "Our whole attitude and outlook upon life will change." You begin to perceive yourself differently. You no longer see yourself as an insecure, inadequate, person with low self-esteem. You have attained higher levels of self-esteem and feel as if you can cope with your world and life situations. Self-esteem can be thought about as having two parts: self-confidence (meaning the belief that you are capable of dealing with your life, and self-worth (which leads you to believe that you are deserving of the good things that life has to offer).

With this change of attitude about life, your fears that you are simply going to be repeating the old destructive

178

cycles disappears. This is stated in the Tenth Promise—
"Fear of people and of economic insecurity will leave us."

The Eleventh Promise states, "We will intuitively know
how to handle situations which used to baffle us." You
learn constructive living. When you are in the habit of self-
destructive living, bad things suddenly happen to you for
no apparent reason because you do things today that produce adverse consequences tomorrow. When the consequences hit, you say, "Why me?"

In recovery, you start living responsibly. You do things
today that produce positive consequences for you tomorrow. Somewhere in the recovery process, you wake up in
the morning and good things start happening to you for no
apparent reason. Now, since you're in the habit of productive problem-solving, you don't have to consciously struggle anymore. You know intuitively what to do and it
becomes automatic.

Finally, the Twelfth Promise says "We will suddenly
realize that God is doing for us what we could not do for
ourselves." By tapping into a bigger frame of reference, a
bigger value system than your addictive self can offer you,
by recognizing a bigger and healthier world view, you find
that you can organize your life around a set of principles
that work better for you. You discover that this enhanced
value system can do things for you that your limited addictive value system could never do.

In short, the Promises tell you that you will change in
four areas: how you think, feel, act, and relate to others. In
terms of thinking, the Promises tell you you are going to
learn how to think clearly, logically, and rationally about
your past life history, your current situation, and your
future plans. In terms of feelings, the Promises tell you that
you will learn how to know what you feel, put it into
words, and communicate it to others. Consequently, you

are able to experience a catharsis and become free of your negative feelings and emotions. You will be able to express your feelings on an ongoing basis. You no longer will have to bottle them up inside, where they cause you constant pain. In terms of actions, the Promises tell you you can break old self-defeating habits that lead to pain. You can learn new, more productive habits that will give you serenity now and in the future. Finally, in terms of relationships, the Promises tell you that you will learn how to relate to other people in your life in a healthy and productive way. As a result, your relationships at work—as well as with friends, family, and lovers—will improve through practicing the Twelve Step principles.

"Are these extravagant Promises?" ask the anonymous recovered authors of the Big Book of A.A. "We think not. They are being fulfilled among us, sometimes quickly, sometimes slowly. They will always materialize if we work for them." The Promises of A.A. tell you where your journey in sobriety will lead you, and the Twelve Steps show you how to get there, one day at a time.

18

GETTING READY
TO ACT

There is an intangible that A.A. calls the "spiritual life," or the spiritual program. A.A. also often uses a corny word—*love*. These are important elements of "the A.A. experience." Something transpires when groups of people, operating on free choice, get together and openly share their reactions, feelings, and opinions about the Twelve Step principles.

There are certain conditions that make this happen—namely, sober people, operating under free choice, discussing the principles that underlie the Steps.

When these conditions occur, something almost "magical" begins to happen. It doesn't happen quickly. It generally takes several weeks for this feeling to emerge in a group. But once people understand how to talk about the A.A. principles and how to be rigorously honest about what they are thinking, feeling, and doing, a spiritual feeling begins to emerge.

A.A., as we have stressed, is a selfish program. What you think and feel counts. As you risk putting your honest, uncensored reactions out there, the A.A. experience begins to happen to you. This experience is not primarily cognitive or behavioral, and this is where A.A. differs from most forms of counseling and therapy.

A.A. doesn't primarily teach rational thinking—although, when you are involved with it for a while, you start to think rationally. A.A. doesn't primarily teach you how to modify your behavior, but if you work the program, your behavior begins to change. It is not a relationship therapy program. A.A. is not primarily designed to fix families or jobs. However, most people who are involved in the fellowship find that their families and jobs do improve.

A.A. is a spiritual program. It is designed to create an experience that makes rigorous honesty, growth, and change possible. This experience is aimed at the feelings and the intuitive sense of what is right and wrong for you, and what is necessary to overcome your addiction and move on to live what is called "the sober life."

This sober life is much more than just not drinking. It also involves finding enduring principles to guide your life that give you meaning and purpose all along the way. Someone once said that ideals are like the stars: "You can never reach them, but you can use them as a guide in getting where you want to go."

The ideals of the A.A. program are like the stars. You are never going to reach them, but, if you are smart, you can use them as guides to steer you in the direction of sobriety. This is why the A.A. program says, "We strive for progress, not perfection." When most people start to listen to the Steps and try to understand what they mean, they say, "What an order! I can't go through with it!" That's right out of Chapter 5 of the Big Book. You cannot work the program perfectly, but you can strive to make progress in understanding the principles and rebuilding your life.

Are you ever going to do a perfect Fourth Step? No. Can you ever do a perfect Fifth Step? No. Is there any benefit in

knowing how to do perfect Fourth and Fifth Steps? Yes.
Why? Because doing them becomes an ideal toward which
you strive, and by striving you change your thinking, behavior, and relationships. By using these principles as
guides in evaluating your behavior, you can change.

You give up the addictive standards against which you
used to measure yourself and you adopt sobriety-centered
standards. You get a new measuring stick against which
you judge the rightness and wrongness of what you do. And
when you get together in your meetings, this is what you
talk about.

"How is it I should live?" "What is 'the good life' now
that I'm not drinking?" "What goals are worthy of attain-
ing?" "What is really good for me in the long run of my
life?" "What is really good for those I love and care
about?" "What mistaken notions do I have about myself
and others that block me from creating what I truly know is
the good life?" "What blocks me from actualizing in my life
these principles that can save my life?"

Most newcomers start looking for magic. There is no
magic in the A.A. program. There are miracles, but they are
not mystical, magical miracles. The miracle is that there are
principles that can make people well and healthy.

If you live according to those principles, you get well; if
you don't, you stay sick. It is all part of a universal law of
consequence. If you understand and apply the principles
correctly, they will work for you. If you distort or misun-
derstand them, they won't work—which means that there
are correct and incorrect interpretations. You can only
know what works or doesn't work by paying close attention to the consequences.

And so you struggle together with your group conscience. You share your opinions. At times, you fight and
disagree, but you do so from a position of love and with the

goal of finding truth. It generally comes out all right in the long run because you are willing to learn and grow. Recovering people call this process "sharing their experience, strength, and hope." They say to one another, "Here's how I interpreted this principle, and here's what I did with it. Here's how I put my understanding of this principle to work in this situation, and here's what happened as a result." And by hearing someone's honest rendition, someone else can then decide, "Do I want to try what they tried?"

If you like the result of what they tried, you do what they did. If you don't like the result they got, you don't. In this way, A.A. is a selfish program: You take what fits you and you leave the rest. There is freedom in this, and that is why I feel so strongly antagonistic toward anyone and anything that is going to create an adverse climate in an A.A. meeting. Freedom is one of the essential ingredients of the Fellowship.

You have the right to come to a meeting and say, "I pass." You have the right not to attend a meeting tonight if you don't want to. You have the right to do what you believe is in the best interest of your recovery, to learn from the consequences, and to come back and talk about what happened for the good or the bad. And you learn from the mistakes of others.

One person may say, "I used to make three meetings a week and I cut down to two a month. Then I went crazy and almost got drunk!" He goes to meetings and he talks about it. Why? Because he is being rigorously honest for his own benefit. And what do other people learn from this?

"Well, gee, maybe if I cut back on my meetings, that's what's going to happen to me." Recovering people know full well that if their "scientific" nature takes over, they may have to do their own experiments.

Do A.A. members have the right to cut down their meeting attendance to two a month if they want to? Yes, they do. But there remains a law of consequences, and there will be a consequence. Can some people stay sober with two meetings a month? Yes, they can. Do other members have the right to tell them that they are working their program wrong? No, they don't. And that's the freedom inherent in A.A.

Now, of course, people fall short of this, and most of them have a hobby of working each other's programs. It's a pastime that's a lot of fun. The *A.A. Grapevine* isn't called that because A.A. members don't gossip. But the bottom line is that the Twelve Step program is based upon freedom of participation. You choose what you will and will not do in your recovery. You decide what you want to use and you decide what you want to leave behind. To move ahead or to lag behind, to attend meetings or not, to select your sponsor or choose not to have a sponsor—these are choices that each member has to make for himself or herself.

Then you pay the price of your choices and share your experiences—good or bad, right or wrong, what worked and what didn't. You evaluate the consequences of your actions with objective people who will help you to be honest with yourself.

This is how the A.A. principles evolved from trial-and-error methods. Alcoholics tried this and it worked; they tried that and it didn't work. And the Twelve Steps are the distilled collective stories of what worked for the early members of A.A. The Twelve Steps evolved from their blood, sweat, and tears. It cost lives to develop these Steps. They are the cumulative experience of literally thousands of people in the early stages of recovery, and I think we need to honor their work.

You can look at A.A. intellectually and say, "This is unscientific." But if you do so, I believe that you are being narrow-minded. A.A. works for many people, and that cannot be denied. It is more productive to ask, "What are the principles that make A.A. work? And how can I learn to bring those principles into my own recovery?" The Twelve Steps are quietly reshaping the face of America because there's valid truth operating within the program. It is that search for the ultimate truth that is the spiritual quest of A.A.

THE TWELVE STEPS OF
ALCOHOLICS ANONYMOUS

1. We admitted we were powerless over alcohol—that our lives had become unmanageable.
2. Came to believe that a Power greater than ourselves could restore us to sanity.
3. Made a decision to turn our will and our lives over to the care of God *as we understood Him.*
4. Made a searching and fearless moral inventory of ourselves.
5. Admitted to God, to ourselves, and to another human being the exact nature of our wrongs.
6. Were entirely ready to have God remove all these defects of character.
7. Humbly asked Him to remove our shortcomings.
8. Made a list of all persons we had harmed, and became willing to make amends to them all.
9. Made direct amends to such people wherever possible, except when to do so would injure them or others.
10. Continued to take personal inventory and when we were wrong promptly admitted it.
11. Sought through prayer and meditation to improve our conscious contact with God *as we understood Him*, praying only for knowledge of His will for us and the power to carry that out.
12. Having had a spiritual awakening as the result of these steps, we tried to carry this message to alcoholics, and to practice these principles in all our affairs.

THE TWELVE TRADITIONS OF ALCOHOLICS ANONYMOUS

1. Our common welfare should come first; personal recovery depends upon A.A. unity.
2. For our group purpose there is but one ultimate authority—a loving God as He may express Himself in our group conscience. Our leaders are but trusted servants; they do not govern.
3. The only requirement for A.A. membership is a desire to stop drinking.
4. Each group should be autonomous except in matters affecting other groups or A.A. as a whole.
5. Each group has but one primary purpose—to carry its message to the alcoholic who still suffers.
6. An A.A. group ought never endorse, finance, or lend the A.A. name to any related facility or outside enterprise, lest problems of money, property, and prestige divert us from our primary purpose.
7. Every A.A. group ought to be fully self-supporting, declining outside contributions.
8. Alcoholics Anonymous should remain forever nonprofessional, but our service centers may employ special workers.
9. A.A., as such, ought never be organized; but we may create service boards or committees directly responsible to those they serve.
10. Alcoholics Anonymous has no opinion on outside issues; hence the A.A. name ought never be drawn into public controversy.
11. Our public relations policy is based on attraction rather than promotion; we need always maintain personal anonymity at the level of press, radio, and films.
12. Anonymity is the spiritual foundation of all our traditions, ever reminding us to place principles before personalities.

ABOUT THE AUTHOR

Terence T. Gorski is the president of The CENAPS Corporation, a training and consultation firm specializing in recovery from addictive disease and relapse prevention therapy. He is a popular speaker and conducts training and workshops in more than twenty different cities each year.

Mr. Gorski is the author of numerous books, audio, and video tapes, including *Passages Through Recovery—An Action Plan for Preventing Relapse, Staying Sober—A Guide for Relapse Prevention, The Staying Sober Workbook,* and *How to Start Relapse Prevention Support Groups.*

He is the clinical director of the National Relapse Prevention Certification School, which trains counselors and therapists in relapse prevention therapy methods.

For information about attending one of his workshops or having Mr. Gorski speak at your conference or conduct presentations for your organization, contact:

The CENAPS Corporation
18650 Dixie Highway
Homewood, IL 60430
708-799-5000